'Ugo Rossi offers a highly original analysis of the current urban condition. The book plays imaginatively on the complex relationships linking cities, neoliberal capitalism and globalization, and extracts from these materials a remarkably informative and incisive diagnosis.'
Allen J. Scott, University of California, Los Angeles

'Reading contemporary global capital from the perspective of the city, Ugo Rossi's *Cities in Global Capitalism* presents a critical geography, rich in analysis and haunted with spectral figures. Rossi shows how the city – the site of historical struggle, artistic and social innovations, and revolutionary uprisings – has been shaped by capital and its state partners with new spatial inequalities, potentialities, and peripheries. As the city once again becomes the destination for the global rich, economic innovation becomes a leading edge of gentrification and the abandoned warehouses of Fordist production become the ghost towers haunting the urban sky – vast areas the mega rich own but rarely inhabit as the ever-expanding homeless below pass by.'
Elizabeth A. Povinelli, Columbia University

'*Cities in Global Capitalism* presents an impressive *tour de force* on the mutually reinforcing relationship between cities, on the one hand, and the capitalist system on the other. Sifting through a wide range of work from across numerous disciplines, Ugo Rossi's account of the contemporary global urban condition is conceptually sophisticated, geographically nuanced and historically sensitive!'
Kevin Ward, University of Manchester

'Ugo Rossi's book is a clear and illuminating overview of the complex relationships between globalized capitalism and urban spaces. A valuable contribution to the project of critically reflecting on our contemporary condition.'
Nick Srnicek, author of *Platform Capitalism* and *Inventing the Future: Postcapitalism and a World Without Work*

Cities in Global Capitalism

Urban Futures series
Talja Blokland, *Community as Urban Practice*
Julie-Anne Boudreau, *Global Urban Politics*
Loretta Lees, Hyun Bang Shin & Ernesto López-Morales
Planetary Gentrification
Ugo Rossi, *Cities in Global Capitalism*

Cities in Global Capitalism —

Ugo Rossi

polity

First published in 2017 by Polity Press

Polity Press
65 Bridge Street
Cambridge CB2 1UR, UK

Polity Press
350 Main Street
Malden, MA 02148, USA

ISBN-13: 978-0-7456-8966-1
ISBN-13: 978-0-7456-8967-8(pb)

A catalogue record for this book is available from the British Library.

Library of Congress Cataloging-in-Publication Data

Names: Rossi, Ugo, 1975- author.
Title: Cities in global capitalism / Ugo Rossi.
Description: Cambridge, UK ; Malden, MA : Polity Press, 2017. | Series: Urban futures
Identifiers: LCCN 2016031538 (print) | LCCN 2016047586 (ebook) | ISBN 9780745689661
  (hardback) | ISBN 9780745689678 (pbk.) | ISBN 9780745689685 (Epdf) | ISBN
  9780745689692 (Mobi) | ISBN 9780745689708 (Epub)
Subjects: LCSH: Urban economics. | Regional economics. | Capitalism. | City-states–Economic
  aspects. | Globalization–Economic aspects.
Classification: LCC HT321 .R674 2017 (print) | LCC HT321 (ebook) | DDC 330.9173/2–dc23
LC record available at https://lccn.loc.gov/2016031538

Typeset in 11.5 on 15 pt Adobe Jenson Pro by Toppan Best-set Premedia Limited
Printed and bound in the UK by CPI Group (UK) Ltd, Croydon

For further information on Polity, visit our website: politybooks.com

Contents

Acknowledgements

While my interest in the transformations of contemporary capitalism – the crisis of Fordism and the transition to post-Fordist societies – dates back twenty years ago now, to the mid-1990s, when I was studying Political Sciences at the University Orientale of Naples, I have been thinking more specifically about the relationship between cities and capitalism over the last six or seven years. I first approached this theme when I received an invitation from the editor of the *Encyclopedia of Urban Studies*, Ray Hutchison, to write two entries: one on the 'capitalist city' and another on 'Manuel Castells' (Rossi, 2010a; Rossi, 2010b). While my previous work had dealt with conceptual issues related to the theorization of urban economic development in post-Fordist and neoliberal times, this invitation led me to systematize my understanding of the evolution of critical urban theory from the 1970s onwards. At the same time, during the last ten years in my research I have been dealing with a set of categorizations, such as the creative city, the smart city and the start-up city, which have stimulated my reflections on the urban realities of contemporary capitalism.

Whereas the ideas presented here draw on this long-term engagement with the conceptualization of post-Fordist capitalism and its relationship to the urban phenomenon, this book has been written over a much more concise period of time, approximately one year, starting in the spring of 2015 and ending in the summer of 2016. During this year, I had the opportunity to share my thoughts as well as to discuss drafts of the chapters of the manuscript with different colleagues and students. In April 2015, I organized a session on the 'urban political in late neoliberalism' at the annual conference of American Geographers in Chicago along with Theresa Enright, who teaches at the University of Toronto in Canada. Theresa has read drafts of some chapters of my manuscript, providing very useful feedback. Over the last few months, with Theresa I have shared reflections on the ambivalence of post-crisis global capitalism and the urban condition, which I have started presenting in this book and would like to develop further in the coming years. In May 2015, I was invited by Bernd Belina to teach a seminar on 'Southern European cities in the global recession' as part of his Master's course on the 'Geographies of Globalization' in the Institute of Human Geography at the Goethe University of Frankfurt, in Germany. My conversations with Bernd, with the other members of the department and with the students enrolled in the seminar provided me with a lively intellectual environment which helped me sharpen my ideas, particularly my understanding of the crisis of 2008, which is at the centre of this book. In Frankfurt I also met Sami Moisio, when we were both visiting the human geography department. In April 2016, Sami invited me to lecture in his urban geography course at the University of Helsinki, in Finland, and to present my work to the department when I was in the very final stages of the writing process. This presentation gave me the opportunity to clarify the structure of the book, particularly the meaning of the terms being used as titles of the chapters.

In December 2015, I presented my research at the geography department of the University of Leuven, Belgium, invited by Manuel Aalbers within the framework of his Master's course on 'the political economy of urban development', taught along with Chris Kesteloot. The political economy environment of Leuven and the provocative questions posed by Manuel and Chris, and by Stijn Oosterlynck of the University of Antwerp (invited as discussant), as well as by the students, helped me clarify my ideas about an understanding of knowledge-intensive capitalism drawing on political economy approaches but also going beyond them. I also thank Manuel for carefully reading different parts of the manuscript, particularly the drafts of chapters 1 and 3.

I am also grateful to Lisa Björkman, of the University of Louisville in the United States, who took the time to read drafts of different chapters of the book and provided important suggestions. With Lisa, in March 2016 I organized a one-week field trip for graduate students in Naples, which focused on the politics of urban infrastructure in post-recession times, particularly looking at the rise of commons-oriented social movements. Her enthusiasm and her 'external' viewpoint on the city in which I grew up and started my academic path have helped me appreciate the importance of studying cities in the South, including the European South, in order to understand contemporary urbanism in today's transitional times. During the field trip in Naples I also exchanged my ideas with Andrea Varriale, who is a PhD student in urban studies at the Bauhaus University of Weimar, in Germany. Andrea generously read my manuscript and provided very useful comments. I also want to thank Lauren Rickards, who teaches at the RMIT University in Melbourne, Australia, with whom I share the editorship of the *Dialogues in Human Geography* journal, particularly its book forum section, for our ongoing conversation about the need for intellectually engaged books in the social sciences and geography most particularly, at a time in which academia increasingly resembles a production line for journal articles.

In Turin, where I am based, I received extensive feedback on the manuscript from Alberto Vanolo and from Anna Paola Quaglia and Samantha Cenere. The latter are my PhD students in the Urban and Regional Development programme of the Politecnico and the University of Turin, where I teach a course on 'critical and reflexive methodologies in urban studies'. With Alberto, we have never stopped exchanging ideas on cities and urban studies since we wrote a book together more than six years ago, whose English-language version is titled *Urban Political Geographies: A Global Perspective* (Rossi and Vanolo, 2012).

Supervising the work of both Anna Paola and Samantha in a relationship of mutual exchange is an important learning opportunity for me, particularly as regards the technology-led transformations of urban economies and societies on which both their dissertations touch.

During the writing process, I benefited tremendously from the support and advice of my editor Jonathan Skerrett, as well as from the criticism and recommendations of three anonymous referees who reviewed the first version of the manuscript. I am also very grateful to Helen Gray, the copy-editor of this book, for her scrupulous and highly competent work on the manuscript. It goes without saying that I am solely responsible for the final outcome. Last, but obviously not least, I dedicate this book to Rebecca, my daughter, who gives me the energy to think beyond today and tomorrow, and to Elisabetta, whose love and intellectual advice are of incommensurable value.

This book is an original piece of work, but in some parts it draws loosely on my previous texts. Earlier and much shorter versions of chapters 2 and 4 were published in Italian in 2014 as 'Gli spazi urbani nell'economia contemporanea' and 'Geografie del capitalism globale' respectively, in a book mainly intended for pedagogical purposes (*Geografia Economica e Politica*), which I co-authored as an individual contributor along with my colleagues at the University of Turin: Sergio Conti, Paolo Giaccaria and Carlo Salone. Chapter 3 in some parts draws on a text entitled 'Neoliberalism' (Rossi, forthcoming), included in a book edited by Mark Jayne and Kevin Ward. The paragraph on the dispossessed city in chapter 5 partly reproduces a section of an article that appeared in *Progress in Human Geography* (Rossi, 2013a).

Introduction

This book explores what is called here the city–capitalism nexus and its political, economic and cultural significance in times of advanced globalization. The close link between cities and capitalism is a relatively recent acquisition. On the one hand, common wisdom has long intuitively described cities as mere physical artefacts, perpetuating the definition dating back to the Enlightenment era, offered by the French *Encyclopédie* (Farinelli, 2003). On the other hand, economists and social scientists have variously theorized capitalism as an economic system based on profit, on the private ownership of the means of production, on market exchange, on wage labour, on the relocation of production outside the home, and on banking institutions founded on credit–debt relations (Ingham, 2008; Hodgson, 2015), but in general have established few or no connections with the urban phenomenon. In the conventional conceptualization of historical capitalism, cities have indeed occupied a relatively marginal place, their role being limited to the invention of financial and commercial techniques in the pre-industrial age and the concentration of a proletarianized workforce at the time of the Industrial Revolution. Now, on the contrary, cities are at the centre of debates over capitalist globalization and everyday life. The professional news outlets as well as the multitudinous social media are literally overwhelmed by accounts of contemporary capitalist economies and societies that base their evidence on what happens in cities and their living environments. Cities are omnipresent in today's public discourse concerning the present and future of global societies, in positive or negative terms: as places of innovation for some (inspiring new technological applications, creative lifestyles, business experiments, etc.); of exploitation for others (reproducing income and wealth imbalances, phenomena of ethno-racial discrimination, etc.). Ambivalent attitudes towards the urban phenomenon reflect those towards capitalism itself, which is a socio-economic system historically vacillating between hope and despair, between a promise of prosperity and development and an experience of inequity and injustice. As a result, in the current 'urban age', as it is customarily defined, cities are no longer viewed merely in relation to, but within capitalism, as its constitutive element.

Why have the fates of cities and capitalism become so inextricable in times of globalization? The present book revolves around this key question. The economic crisis of 2008, in which the interlinkage of housing and finance played a central role, brought about a revival of interest in the long-term and strategic interconnectedness of capital accumulation and financialized urbanization, and particularly in its contradictory manifestations. Is it, therefore, a recurrence of history, a return, in a socio-spatially expanded form, to the pre-industrial age when cities became strongholds of trade and financial power? Or are financialization and the recent financial crisis only a symptom, a crucial manifestation of a deeper involvement of cities in global capitalism? Put briefly, the primary purpose of this book is to accomplish the difficult task of disentangling the city–capitalism nexus in the global age, helping the reader to find satisfactory answers to the aforementioned questions.

VIEWING CITIES IN GLOBAL CAPITALISM

The analysis of the capitalist city has been at the heart of the field of critical urban studies since its first appearance between the late 1960s and the 1970s. Along with the political and intellectual fervour sparked by the student protests that erupted in 1968 in universities across the world (from Berlin, Paris and Rome to Berkeley, New York and Mexico City), and the rise of the 'new left' over the same years, the seminal contributions of Henri Lefebvre, Manuel Castells and David Harvey in the 1970s marked a decisive turning point regarding the ways in which capitalist cities were dealt with in the social sciences. Lefebvre threw light on the emancipatory potential of cities within late capitalist societies, beyond the confrontation between labour and capital, highlighting the inherently political salience of the urban through notions like 'the right to the city' and 'urban revolution'; Castells – laying the foundations for subsequent critical reflections on urban governance – showed how the contemporary city serves as a key site for the management of the capitalist process of social reproduction, coordinating the relationships between the spheres of production, consumption and exchange; finally, Harvey theorized the way in which finance and land rent act as engines of urban growth and socio-spatial transformation, somehow prophesying the financialization of urban development in neoliberal times.

The empiricism and the implicitly anti-urban ideology of the old Chicago School of human ecology were thus left aside by an emerging generation of urban scholars influenced by these leading figures, who gave rise to the so-called 'new urban sociology' and 'radical geography'. Issues of uneven geographical development and socio-spatial justice became central to this new wave of urban scholarship, at a time in which not only student protests but also social movements of unprecedented intensity had taken shape: the anti-colonial liberation movements in the 'third world'; the civil rights mobilizations and the black power movement in the USA; the housing struggles in US and European cities; the anti-dictatorship movements in South America and Southern Europe, where cities were hotbeds of resistance and insurrection (from Buenos Aires to Athens, Barcelona and Lisbon). At the same time, the economic crisis of 1974–5 and the subsequent decline of the Keynesian state and of Fordism-Taylorism as the dominant pattern of industrial organization put an end to the so-called 'golden age of capitalism' of the second post-war decades. During those 'thirty glorious years', as they were also defined (Fourastié, 1979), capitalist societies significantly improved their levels of prosperity, mainly thanks to the process of wealth redistribution brought on by the adoption of welfare-state institutions in Western countries after the end of the Second World War.

The eruption of urban struggles in capitalist cities in the West and beyond, therefore, coincided with the structural crisis of Fordist-Keynesian capitalism in the 1970s. The so-called 'fiscal crisis of the state' (O'Connor, 1973) had heavy repercussions for city governments: New York City's declaration of bankruptcy in 1975 defined an era in twentieth-century urban history. The economic crisis paved the way for an age of austerity that particularly hit cities and regions in mature industrial societies. The urban Fordist cathedrals (such as Turin, Glasgow, Cleveland, Detroit, Pittsburgh, etc.), along with minor industrial centres, witnessed processes of deep socio-spatial restructuring caused by the closure of factories and the relocation of productive activities in areas where fixed costs (land, workforce, taxation) were lower and where social conflict was unknown. This process of capitalist reorganization, along with the weakening of the labour unions, the crisis of the political left and the shift towards a service-oriented economy, led to widespread disillusionment towards Marxism and socialist ideologies within the social sciences, which also affected the field of urban studies. In the 1980s, previous intellectual leaders of progressive urban scholarship, such as Manuel Castells most famously, abandoned Marxism in favour of agency-oriented approaches. Other leading urban theorists, however, such as David Harvey and Edward Soja, persisted in the critique of capitalism, but at the same time got rid of the economism of structuralist Marxism, seriously engaging with the socio-cultural determinants of capitalist change, their relative autonomy and the novel questions posed by gender, ethnicity, race, sexuality and the so-called postmodern condition.

Like other critical social scientists, urban scholars, therefore, started dealing with the intricacies of social and economic life within late capitalist societies, where the economic, the social, the cultural and the political become closely intertwined realms. Marxism, variously understood, was no longer the dominant ideological source of inspiration, but became part of an increasingly pluralistic repertoire of ideas, which comprised a variety of strands of thinking, including feminism, cultural and racial studies, postcolonialism and poststructuralism (from textual deconstruction to the analytics of power), all of them being inspired by 'continental philosophy' and particularly by the so-called 'French theory' (from Derrida to Foucault, Deleuze and Guattari). In this context, late capitalism came to be understood not only as a mode of production based on the private ownership of the means of production and the extraction of surplus value at the expense of the labour force, but also as an intrinsically contradictory moral and societal order in which the socio-spatial segregation of ethnic minorities and the poor coexists with the celebration of difference, and the adoption of technologies of surveillance coexists with the neoliberal embrace of the ideal of freedom. Along these lines, capitalism has been interpreted in close conjunction with the idea of neoliberalism, which has become central to the understanding of the urban experience along with that of globalization. Since the early 1990s, and during the following twenty-five years, urban scholars have looked at the capitalist city through the lenses of globalization and neoliberalism. Today, the study of the city-capitalism nexus cannot be separated from an analysis of globalization and neoliberalism, understood as pervasive forces exerting influence over potentially any aspect of socio-economic life. The 'discovery' of globalization substantially revitalized the field of urban studies from the early 1990s onwards: global-city scholars such as Saskia Sassen, Peter Taylor and Michael Peter Smith helped the field of critical urban scholarship to re-establish a visible presence within not only the social sciences but also within larger debates about the globalizing world in the wider public. The close relationship linking cities to capitalism was now mediated by the consideration of globalization and its capacity to reshape human experience as a whole, including the ways in which capitalism works and is materially organized across the globe. On the other hand, the 'rediscovery' of neoliberalism as a multifaceted force in contemporary societies (beyond its narrow economic formulation as a pro-business policy dismantling the Fordist-Keynesian social compact) has become a distinguishing trait of critical urban studies within the social sciences.

At the turn of the millennium, two major events triggered a change in perspective that also affected the imaginary of critical urban studies: the eruption of the anti-globalization movement in Seattle in 1999 and, only two years later, the September 11 terrorist attacks on the Twin Towers in New York. The former led to the conviction that globalization was not simply another stage in the process of capitalist evolution, but was rather a politico-economic project intimately associated with neoliberalism understood as an ideology of freedom and an 'art of government' naturalizing the logic of the market. While in previous years neoliberalism was associated almost exclusively with Anglo-American countries, primarily the USA and the UK, where in the 1980s the governments of Reagan and Thatcher imposed the new dogmas of privatization, deregulation and individualism, the anti-globalization movement threw light on the neoliberal constitution of globalization and its geographical reach, largely exceeding the confines of the English-speaking world. Neoliberalism as a global project was reinvigorated by the conservative turn that took shape in US politics and in other Western countries after the terrorist attacks of September 2001. The conservative governments of Bush Jr in the USA, Sarkozy in France, Berlusconi in Italy and Merkel in Germany, but also the centrist New Labour government in the UK, gave pre-eminence to ideas of global security and zero tolerance towards the enemies of the West, as well as advocating ownership ideologies, particularly as regards the increase of homeownership rates and the deregulation of the mortgage market as key goals for advanced capitalist societies. A new generation of urban scholars led by Neil Smith, Bob Jessop, Jamie Peck and Neil Brenner, amongst others, drew attention to the urban dimension of neoliberalism, alternatively termed 'urban neoliberalism' or 'neoliberal urbanism', as the defining condition of the contemporary capitalist city.

In many respects, the advent of these new scenarios has distracted attention from the analysis of the capitalist city as such within critical urban scholarship: the contours of the capitalist regime of accumulation, production and consumption have long been taken for granted within contemporary urban studies and the wider critical social sciences, accepting David Harvey's theorization of the urban experience in post-Fordist times (Harvey, 1989a). While acknowledging the absolute relevance of Harvey's theses, this book aims to provide an updated understanding of the current condition of the capitalist city, particularly in the light of the recent Great Recession and its aftermath. It does so by engaging with other strands of thinking within urban studies and the critical human and social sciences, such as neo-institutionalism, cultural political economy, postcolonial urbanism and contemporary radical thought in Italy, but also showing the continued relevance of twentieth-century critical theory, notably that of the Frankfurt School, as a way to illuminate the continuities of contemporary capitalism.

In this book, capitalism is viewed at one and the same time as a force of exploitation and invention, no longer merely incorporating key aspects of society into its system, but encompassing everything, including life itself. The distinctive contribution of this book lies in this understanding of capitalism in relation to the urban phenomenon through explicitly political lenses. While the classic Marxists and other critical social scientists rightly draw attention to the inequalities associated with economic development in urban capitalist societies and the conflictual dimension of the capitalist city, these authors underestimate capitalism's ability constantly to reinvent itself in innovative ways as a response to economic crises and social demands and transformations. On the other hand, institutionalist social scientists as well as spatial economists recognize the societal and governmental dimension of production and innovation, but they draw a veil over the political-strategic dynamic of capitalist economies. In the following chapters, this book will show how urban transformations arise from governmental projects responding to the changing configuration of the capitalist economy. In a context of neoliberal deregulation, the production and expansion of socio-spatial inequality is an inevitable outcome of these transformations.

The tech boom experienced by economically leading cities in the USA and other advanced capitalist economies after the end of the recession of the late 2000s is illustrative of this dynamic. This boom has taken the form of technology-led entrepreneurial communities (the so-called 'start-up phenomenon') particularly concentrating in inner-city areas. This phenomenon has contributed to rejuvenating the capitalist imaginary after the terrible shock of 2008, instilling a renewed sense of entrepreneurial vitality, which is essential for the reproduction of capitalist culture. At the same time, however, this phenomenon has been accompanied by an overheating in housing markets, forcing long-time residents – particularly low-income households of disadvantaged ethnic minorities – to relocate in other cities less exposed to the economic boom but also less attractive in terms of quality of life and job opportunities. Contemporary public policy, as it is premised on neoliberal assumptions of 'thin' interventionism, has proven inadequate to address these social contradictions. Novel social movements and political claims have thus arisen, denouncing growing inequalities of income and wealth and related processes of socio-spatial differentiation.

Consider also the related phenomenon of the technology-based, so-called 'sharing economy', which in the aftermath of the 2008 crisis has undergone a vertiginous growth within consumption sectors typically associated with urban environments, such as housing, transportation, food and education. These economic activities are intended to offer supplementary income opportunities to an impoverished middle class. Moreover, in cultural terms they convey a sense of humane economy based on face-to-face contact and collaboration, giving the illusion of private property as a shareable entity even within capitalist societies. At the same time, however, this technology-based economy throws light on capitalism's tendency to commodify life as a whole, creating new forms of exploitation and self-exploitation. In this context, there is no longer a rigid demarcation between the working place and the private sphere, as there was at the time of historical capitalism. Rather, the domestic space and the private car become directly subsumed within the capitalist circuit of valorization. This makes it hard to measure labour value and productivity: these notions, which are at the heart of the capitalist logic of economic calculation, seem to lose their relevance. Despite this mutating essence of capitalism, in the workplace we are required as never before to improve our performance in line with targets identified by external management consultants, thus acting as entrepreneurs even when we are hired as employees. At the same time, the possibilities offered by digital technologies lead an increasing number of low-paid workers to take advantage of their spare time as an opportunity for seeking out the thrill of being an entrepreneur. The sharing economy is therefore the ultimate manifestation of the rise of the global 'enterprise society' (Lazzarato, 2009). Some cities respond to this burgeoning phenomenon by tightening regulations on temporary rentals and private mobility services, while others adopt a more laissez-faire approach in order to give a boost to their economies. Contradictions, therefore, develop at an intra-urban scale but also at an inter-urban level, reflecting growing inter-regional imbalances within advanced capitalist countries.

As these examples show, the global economic crisis that followed in the wake of the housing crisis and the financial crash of 2007–8 occupies a central place in this book. The late 2000s crisis is important not only as an economic and societal event, but also in intellectual terms, as it has sparked renewed interest in the understanding of the general mechanisms of capitalism, understood as an incessantly evolving entity in the globalized world. The late 2000s crisis, equated by all experts with the major crises in recent capitalist history, particularly with those of the 1930s and the 1970s, has revived classic debates about capitalism and its contradictions, but also about its structural transformations, diversified modes of functioning, and its ability constantly to reinvent its culture as a forward-looking social system. Scholars and commentators seem to agree on the fact that this has been the first truly global crisis in the era of globalization since the regional crises that affected the world economy during the previous fifteen years – to name just the most significant episodes: the economic recession and the currency crisis that hit US and Western European economies (especially Italy, the UK and Spain) respectively in the early 1990s; the Asian and Russian crises of the second half of the 1990s; the bust of the dot-com bubble in the USA in 2000–1; the Argentine default in 2000–1. However, to paraphrase the title of a book on the financial crises of historical capitalism (Reinhart and Rogoff, 2009), 'this time has been different', as the so-called 'great contraction' has involved the world economy as a whole. At the time of writing, in the summer of 2016, the global economy appears a long way from the attainment of macroeconomic stability. Some leading capitalist countries such as the USA and Germany have seemingly left the recession behind, resuming an acceptably positive growth rate, but a persistently stagnant situation continues to characterize the vast majority of advanced economies, especially in Europe. At the same time, non-Western emerging economic powers (the so-called BRICS: Brazil, Russia, India, China, South Africa) have significantly reduced their previous performances, while other previously fast-growing economies are now stuck in recessive spirals, particularly hit in recent years by the burst of the commodities bubble after the boom of the 2000s when the price of raw materials such as fuel and metals constantly rose. It is no surprise, then, that about seven years after the financial crash, Nobel Prize economists of different theoretical orientations (from post-Keynesian Paul Krugman to more mainstream Jacob Hacker and Edmund Phelps) have drawn on former US Treasury Secretary Larry Summers's thesis about the likely advent of an era of 'secular stagnation' caused by insufficient investment demand (Summers, 2014).

The so-called Great Recession, therefore, has been the first structural and global crisis since the advent of neoliberal globalization, understood as a hegemonic politico-economic strategy. However, compared with previous crises in the twentieth century, the recent global recession has apparently not opened the way for a substantial change, neither within capitalism nor within its mode of socio-economic regulation: the crisis of 1929 and the Great Depression of the 1930s marked the crisis of classical liberalism, leading to the advent of Keynesianism, while the crisis of 1974–5 is commonly associated with the start of the post-Fordist transition. Even so, this text will show how, in a context marked by the persistent dominance of neoliberalism, despite its evident failures, contemporary capitalism is not the same as it was back in the time before the Great Recession. The book looks at the way in which, following the 'global recession', capitalism has shifted its focus from the incorporation of society within its value chain to the incorporation of life as such. Cities play a key role in this process, as a consequence of a set of interrelated phenomena taking form in post-recession urban environments: namely, as mentioned earlier, the rise of the so-called sharing and experience economies where the boundaries between production and consumption become increasingly blurred; a second wave of city-based high-tech boom conveying a renewed sense of prosperity and happiness; and the growing exploitation of the cognitive capital of urban societies within the emerging economies of the South at a time of global urbanization. All these phenomena have taken form or intensified since 2009 – the *annus horribilis* of the Great Recession – showing how capitalist urban societies are achieving a 'new normal' after the shock of the financial crisis.

The last few years have been characterized not only by the Great Recession and the subsequent economic impasse, alongside the shaping of novel pathways of capital accumulation, particularly centred on the intensive use of technology, knowledge and communication devices, but also by the resurgence of cities as sites of collective mobilization. From the Arab Spring in Cairo to the Occupy Wall Street protests in New York and the *Indignados* movement in Madrid and Barcelona, from the anti-austerity struggles of Athens to the urban protests in Brazil, from the Gezi Park resistance in Istanbul to the umbrella movement in Hong Kong and the most recent *Nuit Debout* camps in Paris, these movements have brought to the fore issues of social justice, substantive democracy and wealth redistribution with unprecedented strength in the era of globalization. At the same time, contemporary cities offer a rich repertoire of 'minor' contentious geographies, centred on issues in one way or another related to the functioning of capitalist societies and their recent transformations, such as consumption, housing, food and public space. This 'living politics of the city', as Raj Patel has termed it (Patel, 2010), reflects the life-oriented construction of contemporary capitalism as well as its increasingly global scope, in both geographical and societal terms.

CONCEPTUALIZING CITIES IN GLOBAL CAPITALISM

As a consequence of the perceived heightened globalization of the urban experience at a time in which the demographic growth of cities worldwide transforms humans into an 'urban species' (Reba et al.,

2016), a more global approach to urban studies is gaining ground in the field. Postcolonial urban scholars specializing in cities located in the southern hemisphere, such as Ananya Roy and Jennifer Robinson amongst others, have provided a decisive contribution in this direction, openly challenging the West-centrism informing existing urban scholarship. This book largely accepts postcolonial criticism, but it also calls attention to the role of capitalism as the driving force behind global urbanism. In doing so, it suggests looking at the contemporary urban phenomenon through the lens of 'global capitalism', a term that is intended to emphasize in a geographical vein the increasingly planetary reach of the capitalist city, but also in a more qualitative way its tendency to penetrate an ever-growing number of societal realms, constantly deepening the commodification and entrepreneurialization of society.

The evolution and expansion of global capitalism must not be conceived as a linear succession of stages of economic development. This historicist view still permeates influential branches of critical Marxism (Tomba, 2009). Even post-dialectical thinkers like Michael Hardt and Antonio Negri (whose work is a key source of inspiration for this book) overlook capitalism's inconsistencies and historical continuities, presupposing a mono-directional trajectory of development where 'real subsumption' is seen as 'the tendency' of capital. Rather, global capitalism, as understood here, is an intricate process of spatio-temporal stratification, characterized by the juxtaposition of a variety of development pathways, hegemonic projects, forms of life and historical temporalities. At the same time, the engagement in this book with the increasingly global dimension of urbanization and urbanism is not intended to uncritically embrace universalism in the analysis of the contemporary city–capitalism nexus – the account provided here is inevitably situated, forged by the author's positionality. As Benedetto Croce once wrote about the impossibility of universal history: 'history is thought, and, as such, thought of the universal, of the universal in its concreteness, and therefore always determined in a particular manner' (Croce, 1921: 60).

This book, therefore, aims to highlight the central contribution provided by cities to the multifaceted experience of 'global capitalism' in the contemporary world. It does so by embracing a narrative strategy that requires dealing with the past in close relationship to the present (the Foucauldian idea of the 'history of the present') and with 'the present as history', in order to make sense of the living dimension of the city-capitalism nexus at a time of biopolitics where life is central to the dynamics of cities, capitalism and their mutual dependence. To put it with Roberto Esposito, the proposed analysis is based, on the one hand, on a deep engagement with 'the unfolding of the most pressing current events' and at the same time on the identification of 'dispositifs that come with a long or ancient history' (Esposito, 2012: 5). The latter are identified here with the key forces that have nurtured the city–capitalism nexus over the centuries, such as financial power, entrepreneurialism and cognitive capital, coming to the fore in the current 'urban age' of capitalist globalization. This intentionally 'presentist' stance demands attention be paid to the various stories of the living entities that contribute to the experience of the city-capitalism nexus. Such stories are always under way and indeterminate in their outcome, preventing any attempt at a universal account of this nexus where everything could be fitted into one predefined, overarching tendency. At the same time, this 'living understanding' is inherently political, with the political embedded in existing power structures (Esposito, 2016), such as those of 'global capitalism'. From the perspective of this text, this means also that political alternatives to capitalism are found within the functioning of capitalism itself, as will be seen when the book will touch on recent post-capitalism theses.

The book thus investigates the global configuration of the contemporary city–capitalism nexus, understood as a juxtaposition of historical, geographical, societal, cultural and economic interactions. This work seeks to convey the complexity of global capitalism in its urban form – the variously central roles played by such different forces as financialization, institutional capacity, innovative entrepreneurship, the housing sector, consumption, technology and the cultural economy. Even though they can be considered autonomous entities, these forces are also interrelated. Moreover, none of these forces is considered to be superior to the others in terms of influence over the urban phenomenon. Customarily, urban scholars investigating the city–capitalism relationship tend to privilege one sector over the others: Marxists influenced by the work of David Harvey and his theory of the secondary circuit of capital will tend to emphasize the financialization of urban development and the role of real-estate business as the driving force behind contemporary urban dynamics (Harvey, 2012; Krätke, 2014); mainstream urban economists proposing a theorization of cities as creative environments particularly focus on the urbanization of innovative entrepreneurship and labour (Florida, 2012; Moretti, 2012); and, finally, social critics interested in the changing cultures of capitalist cities look at the colonization of urban lifestyles induced by the renewed forces of consumerism and gentrification (Zukin, 2010). This book deliberately avoids a univocal understanding of capitalism and the city in times of advanced globalization, its main goal being to explore from a global perspective the different ways – both negative and affirmative – in which contemporary capitalism shifts towards the incorporation of life itself into its accumulation structures. This includes a consideration of what cities have to offer in this ambivalent characterization of global capitalism: from financialization that exploits society while socializing ownership, to the emergent technology-based economies simultaneously using everyday life as a site of exploitation and reinvention. As Timothy Campbell (2008) has summarized, the negative dimension of governmental action illustrates the politics *over* life originally investigated by Foucault, when he coined the notions of biopolitics and biopower that in more recent times have been reconceptualized by Agamben in his theory of the state of exception. The affirmative dimension, on the other hand, can be seen as the politics *of* life where the idea of production refers to the production of subjectivity and relational forms of life rather than of goods and services.

In order to make sense of the plurality of socio-economic forms (and forms of life) characterizing global capitalism, the book combines various intellectual frameworks which still inform critical social science: the classic Marxists look at how culture is shaped by the economy, while the neo-institutionalists think that historically given institutional configurations exert decisive influence over the trajectories of economic development; urban political economists, who constitute a major branch within critical urban studies, bring together the Marxist and the institutionalist traditions. The book establishes more than a dialogue with these 'traditions', as in several parts it derives its analytical tools and interpretive frameworks directly from them. At the same time, the text also goes beyond these established strands within urban scholarship, by engaging with authors who have approached the study of contemporary societies from a materialist-ontological perspective – notably Michael Hardt and Antonio Negri, Giorgio Agamben, and Paolo Virno, authors inspired by a heterogeneous set of Western critics of modernity that includes Spinoza and Deleuze, Nietzsche and Heidegger, Benjamin and Arendt. These authors have investigated ontology beyond metaphysics, looking at the materiality of the living being in capitalist societies, particularly regarding language, the body and emotions. The work of these authors allows us to navigate the fluctuating forms of life generated by contemporary capitalism at a time in which life itself becomes increasingly incorporated into the mechanics of capitalist cities in both negative and affirmative ways. In contemporary capitalism, the economic becomes inextricable from the cultural, the institutional, the social and the biological. From this perspective, even Althusser's refusal of conventional dialectical thinking which posits the countless number of intersected determinations on the capitalist economy (Althusser, 2010) appears insufficient, as it is still premised on the distinction between structure (the economic base of capitalist societies) and superstructure (the cultural expression of the former). The idea of determination (and its pluralistic version, over-determination; see Jameson, 2010) is replaced here by that of 'immanence' (Deleuze and Guattari, 1987), particularly as has been revisited by Hardt and Negri (2000), as a way to overtake the constraints of dialectical thought. Drawing on Hardt and Negri's approach, this book analyses the urban phenomenon in a relationship of immanence with global capitalism understood as an 'ontological machine' creating new subjectivities through relations of both subjection and enlivenment. Any principle of external causality is untenable from this perspective, as the idea of immanence entails the fact that the different entities being analysed here (the city, the global economy, neoliberalism, urban societies) are integral parts of global capitalism: they cannot stand outside it. This 'being part' is not univocal, but intrinsically multidirectional in both temporal and spatial terms. Capitalism is fundamentally an urban phenomenon, whose constitutive elements (the 'key forces' mentioned earlier) trace their roots back particularly to the medieval period, having acquired renewed significance in the current global age, as will be shown in chapter 1. Rather than merely being a set of ideas adopted by the public-policy sphere in the dominant centre of the global economy (Anglo-America) and then circulated by its politico-economic elites across the world, neoliberalism is considered here as an entity that has grown into the living tissue of the global capitalist city. A critique of the policy-mobility paradigm and the variegated-neoliberalization thesis, where neoliberalism is viewed as an elite-led external force circulating across the globe, originating from 'somewhere' and being exported 'elsewhere', will be provided along these lines. In highlighting the living dimension of the city–neoliberalism nexus, this book shows how the entrepreneurialization of society and the self, which is at the heart of advanced liberal societies, is inscribed within global capitalism. This living dimension manifests itself autonomously, but at the same time requires governmental action in order to be organized as a system, thus highlighting the importance of analysing public policy and the underlying politico-economic strategies and the ways in which these comply with the material constitution of capitalist societies.

Over the last fifteen years, capitalist societies have been particularly characterized by the confrontation between the logic of dispossession associated with neoliberal governmentality, which the financial crash of 2008 and the subsequent wave of austerity urbanism have normalized, and the production of new subjectivities and relational forms of life in response to the cultural crisis of capitalism, epitomized by the increased entrepreneurialization of society and the self enabled by digital technologies. This ambivalence is reflected in the different, and irreconcilable, political scenarios taking shape at the global level. Post-crisis societies witness the resurgence of a transformational conception of politics, based on relations of equality and solidarity, in which cities are privileged sites for commons-oriented movements contesting austerity-driven politics. At the same time, post-crisis societies face the risk of a return of new forms of fascism giving voice to the 'bad new' – as Paolo Virno calls it (Joseph, 2005) – arising from the current condition of frustration and social anger experienced by the middle class, which foments individualism and intolerance towards ethno-cultural minorities, and which is partly a reaction against the delusion of community in the post-recession capitalist economies. This situation particularly characterizes Western societies, which have been the epicentre of the global economic crisis, but it is likely to extend to the emerging economies of the planet as they experience a precipitous slowdown in their economic performances and a growing crisis of legitimacy affecting their elites.

OVERVIEW OF THE BOOK

This work consists of five chapters. Each chapter is illustrative of a specific social dynamic through which cities become enmeshed in global capitalism. The first chapter is constructed around the idea of 'emergence'. The chapter identifies three 'emergences' within the city–capitalism long-term relationship: financial power, entrepreneurialism and cognitive capital. It is argued that these distinctive features are products of the historical trajectory of capitalist urbanism: they are not creations of the contemporary age, but have to be viewed as long-standing features of capitalist cities resurfacing and becoming generalized in a context of globalization. This chapter is therefore not intended to provide a historical reconstruction of the capitalist city in the conventional sense. It is, rather, conceived as a 'history of the present', to use a phrase of Michel Foucault's. Through this 'history', attention is drawn to the process of selection and retention of social phenomena (finance, institutional capacity, knowledge) which function as foundational moments to capitalism at different times of its historical trajectory: from the medieval period, in which city-republics in Western Europe played a central role in the rise of both the financial sector and of a sense of municipal civicness, up to contemporary projects of social transformation aiming to turn marginalized urban areas such as the slums of Southern megacities into clusters of entrepreneurial inventiveness. The forces of finance, civicness and knowledge which define the condition of capitalist urbanism over the long term, this chapter shows, have appeared first as phenomena associated with specific cities and urban areas, and then have been turned into 'processes', through their geographical dissemination and reproduction in a wide range of socio-economic domains. This transmutation of phenomena into processes has culminated with the advent of neoliberal globalization, which has allowed the generalization of the capitalist city as the dominant socio-spatial form on the planet.

The second chapter – entitled 'extensions' – looks at the first component of neoliberal globalization: the global. It does so by examining the various stages of the scholarly debates concerning the relationship between cities and globalization, reviewing territorial, networked and relational understandings, as well as critically assessing recent theses about global urbanism and planetary urbanization. This chapter shows how scholars have gradually shifted their focus of attention from the structural determinants of the global-city phenomenon towards an extended conceptualization of the global dimension of our urban experience. With reference to recent theses about policy mobility and planetary urbanization, the chapter highlights their merits, but also their limitations, providing a sympathetic critique of these highly influential strands of research within current urban scholarship dealing with cities and globalization, in order to move beyond them in the remainder of the book.

The third chapter – entitled 'continuities' – is dedicated to analysing the second component of neoliberal globalization: neoliberalism and its relationship of immanence with the capitalist city. As mentioned earlier in this introduction, rather than seeing neoliberalism as a mere set of ideas and an elite-led external force circulating across the globe, the city–neoliberalism nexus is understood here as an inner relationship of continuous interchange, whose global dominance has put an end to the 'Keynesian exception' of the post-war decades. On the one hand, neoliberal urbanism has appropriated pre-existing features of capitalist urbanism, such as the relentless intensification of mass consumption and the expansion of homeownership as an ideology of private property, which is behind the housing and financial crash of 2007–8. On the other hand, contemporary neoliberal urbanism has absorbed within itself social phenomena that were previously separate from profit-driven economic valorization, notably those of creativity. In an era of advanced globalization, the adoption of a neoliberal governmentality is key to the propagation of norms, mores or standards that are conducive to the sorts of lifestyle that arise from the entrepreneurialization of society and of the self.

The idea of 'propagation' leads us to the fourth chapter, 'diffusions'. The chapter shows how homogenization processes resulting from the global phenomena of capitalist colonization, such as McDonaldization, Disneyfication and Guggenheimization, are not merely to be understood as straightforward uniformization of the urban experience but – drawing on the insights of postcolonial urbanists – as a continuous overlapping of unique and repetitive processes at the same time, reflecting place-specific hegemonic projects as well as changing capitalist configurations. The chapter reconstructs the geographies of global capitalism as seen through the lenses of these culturally hegemonic forces and the place-sensitive receptions of global processes. Rather than interrogating the forms of consumption associated with these forces, as sociologists of postmodernity have done in previous years, this chapter looks at their propagation across the globe as a process of capitalist colonization: a 'civilizing process', as defined by Norbert Elias. This is simultaneously understood as a transformation of human behaviour in public space, as in Elias's original sense, and as a process of governance experimentation that bypasses existing planning regulations while introducing novel spatial arrangements aligned with the neoliberal rationality of government

The fifth chapter of the book is dedicated to an analysis of the 'variations' of the global capitalist city under conditions of neoliberal dominance. The chapter offers an illustration of the rapidly evolving nature of contemporary capitalism in its urban form, identifying three subjective figures of the capitalist city before and after the global economic crisis of the late 2000s: the socialized city, the dispossessed city and the revenant city. The socialized city reflects the process of subsumption of society characterizing the post-Fordist transition within globalizing capitalist societies: this involves the formation of a 'socialized' workforce, particularly epitomized by the rise of urban creative

economies. But the socialization process is not limited to this phenomenon, as the valorization of language, affects and diffused knowledge involves the entire social fabric, not just the knowledge-intensive
sectors of the workforce, as this chapter argues. The dispossessed city
is understood as a normalized 'state of exception', brought about on
the one hand by the global expansion of capitalism and on the other
hand by the global financial crisis and the subsequent wave of austerity.
The condition of being dispossessed thus becomes a defining feature
of contemporary capitalist cities at a time of normalized austerity
urbanism with deepening socio-spatial inequalities. Finally, the revenant city (a term borrowed from Alejandro G. Iñárritu's recent film,
The Revenant) is the outcome of processes of societal re-enlivenment
within the latest phase of post-recession capitalist development, in
which life as such has been increasingly subsumed within the capitalist
value chain. The advent of the web 2.0 and of the experience economy
is particularly illustrative of these trends, which some authors interpret
as indicative of incipient post-capitalist transformation of our societies, as this chapter shows. This incorporation of life into the cultural
circuit of capitalism is the way in which contemporary cities have
reacted to the 'great contraction' of the late 2000s in affirmative ways.
Like the main character of *The Revenant*, city dwellers are at one and
the same time victims and victimizers in this process of survival. The
process of capitalist regeneration based on the economization of life
that has followed the global economic crisis of the late 2000s leads an
increasing number of city dwellers to embark on business experiments
involving a mobilization of the self: in doing so, this chapter argues,
they combine two mutually excluding modes of being, such as those
of community and individualization. This ambivalent and inherently
contradictory process of societal entrepreneurialization leads cities
to alter their socio-ecological metabolism, as weaker groups such as
older or low-income residents are those affected by the revamping of
housing markets, the financialization of everyday life and the shrinkage

of traditional economic circuits (from small retail business in cities in the North to the informal economy in cities in the South) customarily associated with the emerging 'biopolitical economies' in neoliberal contexts, as mentioned earlier in this introduction.

Finally, in recapitulating the main arguments of the previous chapters, the book concludes with a reflection on the ambivalence of the urban condition in the current context of the widespread turbulence affecting global capitalism, with its contradictory political implications, vacillating between 'the ever-given possibility of fascism' (to borrow a term by Karl Polanyi) led by an increasingly frustrated middle class and the resurrection of a solidarity-based approach to social relations, as in the case of commons-oriented social movements. The latter is particularly exposed to the risk of being absorbed into the mainstream of capitalist discourse, particularly when its political salience remains inarticulate, the chapter concludes.

1 Emergences

CITIES IN CAPITALISM: A HISTORY OF THE PRESENT

Despite having been marginally included in standard economic analysis, it is widely recognized now that urbanism (i.e., the way of life of city dwellers) and urbanization (i.e., the expansion of urban environments) are essential components of the capitalist process. This chapter focuses on the long-term interdependence between cities and capitalism; a link that has become increasingly inextricable in present-day societies. Certainly, capitalism could not exist without cities, as over the centuries its rise, consolidation and evolution have been intimately associated with the functioning of urban societies, their distinctive characteristics and changing trajectories. Contrary to the conventional wisdom that has long viewed cities merely as manufacturing centres and reservoirs of the workforce, it is now widely acknowledged that cities have provided a far more decisive contribution to capitalism, particularly to its pre-industrial stages as well as to the current globalization era.

In the era of globalization the importance of cities is reasserted in different ways, as the second chapter of this book will show in greater detail. Globalization, particularly in the multicentric forms characterized by the relentless expansion of urbanization and the coexistence of different hegemonies across the planet, has led historical emergences to re-surface with unprecedented intensity. In particular, this chapter identifies three historical 'emergences': financial power, entrepreneurialism and cognitive capital. These are the key forces – this book maintains – that have been brought to the fore within the contemporary round of capitalist globalization. Capitalism today is simultaneously based on the multiplication of financial activities, on the entrepreneurialization of society and on the incorporation of knowledge and affects into the circuit of production. This combination of finance, entrepreneurialism and knowledge is at the heart of the leading role played by cities in today's capitalist world: cities' relationship with finance is particularly epitomized by the prominence of real-estate and mortgage sectors; cities' entrepreneurialism is expressed in the form of entrepreneurial governance, but also of wider entrepreneurialization of the self within advanced liberal societies; and, finally, in an advanced era of knowledge-based capitalism, characterized by the adoption of information and communication devices based on social interaction (the so-called Web 2.0), cities become central sites of knowledge creation. This centrality is due in large part to the intensity of socio-affective relations which exceed the boundaries of the institutions formally dedicated to the process of innovation, such as a firm's research and development division.

This chapter will look at the ascendancy of these forces, with the purpose of interrogating the current urban condition in its intimate association with global capitalism. In doing so, the chapter will show how the present age of neoliberal globalization has widened the reach of these three long-standing forces. The chapter is divided into three sections. The first section will look at how the phenomenon of financialization, whose roots date back to proto-capitalist European cities, has expanded socially, permeating every aspect of social life and, ultimately, life itself. The second section will show how urban entrepreneurialism has capitalized on long-standing socio-cultural features of urban environments, enabling cities to engage with the local–global dialectic in the early stages of contemporary globalization and a larger set of socio-spatial relations in the more recent context of multi-centric globalization. The third section will discuss how in contemporary knowledge-based economies the cognitive capital that is historically associated with the succession of capitalism's socio-technical paradigms exceeds the confines of the capitalist firm and other formalized economies entities, becoming a ubiquitous social dynamic rooted in a variety of urban environments. Finally, the concluding section of the chapter will further clarify the use of the notion of 'emergences'.

In short, this chapter is not intended to provide a history of the capitalist city in the conventional sense, but should be understood as a 'history of the present' in the Foucauldian sense, whose purpose is to prepare the ground for the deeper exploration of 'cities in global capitalism' that will be offered in the subsequent chapters of the book.

FINANCIAL POWER

While the appearance of the urban phenomenon precedes that of capitalism, as urban forms of coexistence have marked the history of mankind since the time of the ancient Greek *polis*, capitalism cannot exist without cities. This mutual relation of dependence has long-standing roots. As Belgian historian Henri Pirenne first contended, the formation of capitalism was originally associated with the ascent of cities in Western Europe and their entrepreneurial classes in the Middle Ages. In particular, Pirenne thought that the essential features of capitalism – such as individual enterprise, credit, commercial profits, speculation, etc. – could already be found from the twelfth century onwards in the Italian city-republics of Florence, Genoa and Venice, as well as in other economically leading European cities, particularly those of the Low Countries, such as Ghent and Bruges in today's Flanders (Pirenne, 1956).

In subsequent decades, Pirenne's long-term perspective was revived by scholars – particularly interdisciplinary historians and sociologists – embracing the so-called *longue durée* approach to the study of human societies: first, the exponents of the French *Annales* school of social and economic history and, in more recent times, the proponents of world-systems analysis in the USA. Amongst the former, Fernand Braudel systematized Pirenne's thesis, arguing that capitalist forms of accumulation started in thirteenth-century Italy with the rise of city-states. In putting forward this thesis, Braudel has been the first scholar to introduce the idea that capitalism is not just a mode of production, as the conventional Marxists had hitherto maintained. Rather, capitalism has to be understood as a mode of rule and accumulation, most notably as a monopoly power over market forces and as a historically evolving economic process based on the realization of profit and the accumulation of wealth. In his view, during the modern age cities played a central role in the formation of market economies and related forms of civilization across the Mediterranean (Braudel, 1983). This view has exerted strong influence over the contemporary understanding of global or world cities. In particular, drawing inspiration from Braudel, geographer Peter Taylor – a leading proponent of world-city research in the last two decades – has argued that, as concentrations of business services, contemporary world cities are crucial to the reproduction of capitalist monopoly powers based on the generation of knowledge and expertise necessary for the functioning of the world economy (Taylor, 2000). In a previous writing, reflecting on London's renaissance since the late 1980s as a global financial centre within a national context marked by the economic decline of the United Kingdom, Taylor saw the ascendancy of world cities in the contemporary era of globalization as another chapter in the long-term 'cities vs states' rivalry. In the modern age, Taylor noted, the rise of territorial states since the late sixteenth century has occurred in response to the decline of Antwerp and Genoa, at that time the two leading trade and financial centres of the international economy, whose destiny became dependent on that of the Spanish Empire. However, the dominance of Amsterdam took shape under the protective umbrella of the newly established

United Provinces (the independent 'Dutch Republic'), which gave rise not only to the 'Dutch golden age' in economic terms, but also to the lasting pre-eminence gained by the sovereign nation-state after the peace of Westphalia in the mid-seventeenth century (Taylor, 1995). In the 1990s, the advent of the era of globalization, characterized by powerful world cities and apparently disempowered nation-states, has been widely perceived as a return to a pre-Westphalian era (see chapter 2).

An interpretation of the city–capitalism long-term relationship predicated on the idea of financial hegemonies is particularly due to the work of Giovanni Arrighi. Drawing on Pirenne and Braudel, and more directly inspired by the work on world-systems theory by Immanuel Wallerstein with whom he collaborated in the Fernand Braudel Research Centre in the USA, Arrighi further developed the idea that the rise of capitalism is not to be associated with that of nation-states, as the conventional wisdom has long held, but with that of city-states as condensations of powerful financial institutions. In his book, Arrighi identified 'four systemic cycles of accumulation': namely:

> a Genoese cycle, from the fifteenth to the early seventeenth centuries; a Dutch cycle, from the late sixteenth century through most of the eighteenth century; a British cycle, from the latter half of the eighteenth century through the early twentieth century; and a US cycle, which began in the late nineteenth century and has continued into the current phase of financial expansion. (Arrighi, 1994: 6)

According to Arrighi, each cycle of accumulation consists of the alternation of a phase of material expansion, when trade and production expand in search of new geographical routes and economic sectors, and a subsequent phase of financial reinvestment, which takes place when profitable opportunities in the trade and industrial sectors are shrinking. In particular, Arrighi believes that city-states have played a central role in the first two cycles of capital accumulation, before the advent of the nation-state and what is customarily known as the Industrial Revolution of the eighteenth and nineteenth centuries, when cities became manufacturing centres and reservoirs of the industrial proletariat.

While having already pointed to the 1980s as a phase of financialization following the crisis of over-accumulation in the previous decade, which affected Western capitalism and particularly the US-centred regime of accumulation, in subsequent writings Arrighi has confronted his interpretation of historical capitalism with David Harvey's conceptualization of post-Keynesian capitalism and the changing trajectories of capital accumulation after the economic crisis of the 1970s, particularly with his theses about the three circuits of capital, about capital's need for new spatio-temporal fixes, and with his more recent idea of accumulation by dispossession (Arrighi, 2004 and 2009). Harvey's theory of the three circuits of capital builds on the assumption that conditions of over-accumulation in the production and trade sectors (the primary circuit of capital) lead to flows of capital into the secondary circuit (real estate, physical infrastructure and the built environment) and the third circuit (research, higher education and development), mediated by the state (through large-scale real-estate projects and the increase of social expenditure) and financial institutions (through financial investment) (Harvey, 1978). In his theory of the secondary circuit of capital, David Harvey elaborated on an original formulation provided by Henri Lefebvre a few years earlier in his pathbreaking *La Révolution Urbaine*:

As the principal circuit – current industrial production and the movable property that results – begins to slow down, capital shifts to the second sector, real estate. It can even happen that real-estate speculation becomes the principal source for the formation of capital, that is, the realization of surplus value. As the percentage of overall surplus value formed and realized by industry begins to decline, the percentage created and realized by real-estate speculation and construction increases. The second circuit supplants the first, becomes essential. (Lefebvre, 2003: 160)

In Harvey's view, over-accumulation crises are dealt with not only through switching flows of capital (from production and trade to the built environment and knowledge-intensive sectors) but also through new spatio-temporal fixes (originally defined only as 'spatial fix': Harvey, 1982), allowing better conditions for investment and profitability via a spatial and temporal deferral (Harvey, 2003).

Harvey's theory of over-accumulation has become largely dominant in Marxist-oriented human geography and urban studies: an uncontested orthodoxy, according to a sympathetic critic (Holgersen, 2015). This theory, originally formulated between the second half of the 1970s and the first half of the 1980s, has witnessed a revival in recent years, in the context of the global financial crisis that impacted capitalist economies in 2008, leading to the so-called 'great contraction': the first truly global crisis since the advent of globalization. Prior to the financial crash, the housing sector acted as a catalyst of an otherwise slow-growth capitalist economy, in the USA as well as in more peripheral and smaller, but also growing, economies such as the Baltic countries, Spain and Ireland. Since the early 2000s, shortly after the burst of the Internet bubble and the shock of the terrorist attacks in the USA, the continuation of capital accumulation has become increasingly dependent on a wave of financial speculation closely linked to the real-estate sector. The deregulation of the mortgage sector led the property sector to expand, becoming one of the main factors in the larger process of financialization that the world economy has witnessed in the last three decades, as well as a major source of household indebtedness (Marazzi, 2010). David Harvey and the scholars embracing his theoretical framework have repeatedly underlined the 'urban roots' of the recent global economic crisis, stressing the intimate link between cities and financialization in neoliberalized capitalist societies: the definition of 'subprime cities' (derived from the subprime mortgages whose default initially caused the financial crash in the USA) is particularly illustrative of the finance-city isomorphism in contemporary societies (Aalbers, 2012).

Financialization has therefore become a distinguishing trait of the contemporary stage of capitalist development in the USA and elsewhere in the world economy, particularly from the 1970s onwards after the end of the post-war golden age of capitalism and with the shift towards neoliberal globalization (Krippner, 2005). The financialization phenomenon can be observed from at least three different perspectives: first, as in Arrighi's work, as a regime of capital accumulation, sustained by the recurrent increase of profits derived from financial activities rather than from productive investment; second, as a mechanism underlying the functioning of the contemporary capitalist corporation, as a consequence of the importance acquired by the so-called 'shareholder value' (particularly benefiting managers, shareholders and employees) within business practices over productive goals, such as the increase of employment and the realization of new investment opportunities; and, third, as a force pervading an ever-growing number of realms of social life, such as housing (securitization of mortgages), consumption (growth of consumer credit) and social protection (private pension funds), centred on the idea of the citizen as a risk-taking and self-managed investor (van der Zwan, 2014).

The advent of financialization, particularly in its third dimension (the financialization of the everyday and of life itself: Martin, 2002; Lazzarato, 2012; Joseph, 2014), deserves attention as it directly involves the changing role of cities in the context of contemporary capitalism. Since the decline of Keynesianism and post-war capitalism, the city is no longer a locus of mediation between conflicting actors (the working class and the ruling class) and site of redistribution and allocation of government spending (Castells, 1977). Nor can it any longer be viewed

exclusively as a terrain of realization of surplus value created by conditions of over-accumulation, as in Lefebvre and Harvey's theory of
the secondary circuit of capital. The analysis of the capitalist city
centred on Harvey's conceptual framework powerfully captures the
structural dynamic of contemporary urbanization, but it does not illuminate the substantive changes undertaken by capitalism as a regime
of biopolitical control in recent times, particularly as a consequence
of the powerful role played by neoliberalism as a mobile government
technology (Ong, 2007). A key effect of the deep neoliberalization of
the urban environment is that the capitalist logic has widened its reach
by subsuming the lives of urban residents within the intrinsic mechanisms of financial capitalism (Rossi, 2013b). Financialization turns
city residents simultaneously into exploited, over-indebted entities and
into potentially entrepreneurial subjects. This is a key manifestation
of the ambivalent condition of contemporary capitalism – where the
exploitation and the productive mobilization of life coexist – that this
book intends to bring to the attention of readers.

In this sense, today's neoliberal hegemony should not be understood
merely as a return to a market-led governance of economies and societies. In the concluding section of his *The Long Twentieth Century* masterpiece, Giovanni Arrighi interpreted the revival of free-market ideas
– epitomized by the dominance of neoliberal ideas in the Western
world from the 1980s onwards – as a manifestation of the long-term
alternation of phases of 'economic freedom' and 'economic regulation',
according to Henri Pirenne's terminology. However, the evolution of
neoliberalism and its role in deepening cities' association with capitalism invites us to see it not merely in terms of return but in the sense
of a more advanced regime of control: in one word, of 'biopower', to
put it in Michel Foucault's terms (Foucault, 1990). As Foucault argued
in his influential lectures on neoliberal governmentality at the Collège
de France (Foucault, 2008), while classic liberalism had called on government to respect and monitor market freedom, in the neoliberal

approach the market started being viewed as the organizing and regulatory principle underlying the state itself (Lemke, 2001). This means that the logic of the capitalist market was bound to permeate all aspects of social life, according to the emerging neoliberal wisdom. Writing in the aftermath of the 1929 crisis, Karl Polanyi saw capitalist usage of land, money and labour as fictitious commodities during the time of classic liberalism in the nineteenth century (Polanyi, 2001). Today, through the socialization of financial mechanisms (see chapter 5), the biopolitical stage of contemporary capitalism has transformed life itself into an ambivalent site of capital valorization.

Along these lines, fusing Foucault's lesson with ideas derived from neo-Marxian thinking, which reinterprets Marx's notion of real subsumption and views capitalism as a 'social factory', it can be argued that the latest tide of financialization has led to a biopolitical stage of urban development based on the subsumption of 'life itself' through indebtedness in key aspects of city life, such as housing, education and consumption (Marazzi, 2010; Lazzarato, 2012). This issue is discussed in more depth in chapters 3 and 5 when the contours of contemporary neoliberalism and its interchanges with the contemporary capitalist city are explored.

ENTREPRENEURIALISM

While Pirenne, Braudel and Arrighi have attracted attention on the economic-political factors in the rise of medieval city-states in northern Italy and particularly on the dynamics of wealth accumulation, illuminating the role of cities as concentrations of financial power, the linkage between pre-industrial capitalism and the rise of city-states in central and northern Italy during the Middle Ages has been theorized from a socio-cultural perspective by Robert Putnam. A mainstream political scientist, he is widely known for his pioneering contribution to the theorization of a key concept in contemporary social science: the notion of social capital. While Putnam theorized social capital in a book assessing the decline of associationalism in contemporary US society (Putnam, 2000), in his previous book on the performance of local government in contemporary Italy he proposed to use the closely related concept of 'civicness' (Putnam, 1993). Using this concept, Putnam argued that a key factor in the long-standing north–south divide in Italy has its origins in the medieval period when centre-north Italy saw the rise of the communes and a vibrant city life, which favoured the development of social relations based on mutual trust, horizontality and a widespread sense of civicness, while southern regions remained subjected to the autocratic rule of the Normand kingdom, where vertical relations of patron–client were prevalent.

These socio-cultural factors were decisive in the ascent of primordial forms of capitalism and place-based entrepreneurialism in the Italian communes: the invention of credit due to banks located in medium-sized cities in the Italian centre-north was enabled by such relations of trust, Putnam argues. Despite the unravelling of the communal republics, Italian centre-northern regions preserved their distinguishing features of civicness, trust and cooperation within an increasingly competitive environment. The way in which another mainstream political scientist, Francis Fukuyama, whose idea of the 'end of history' after the collapse of Soviet socialism was particularly influential in the 1990s, has made use of the concept of social capital helps clarify Putnam's interpretation. Fukuyama emphasizes the value of trust in contemporary capitalist societies and the related virtues of reciprocity, moral obligation and duty towards community, contending that economic development is not just based on rational calculation and impersonal managerial structures, as was the case at the time of Fordist capitalism and Weberian sociology (Fukuyama, 1997). From his perspective, the failure of both Fordism and the associated mode of regulation, Keynesianism, should be ascribed to capitalism's eradication from community-based relations.

The flexible specialization phenomenon and the related resurgence of regional economies in post-Fordist times brought to light a unique combination of competition and collaboration within highly specialized productive systems, such as those of Silicon Valley, the regions of the so-called 'third Italy' (the centre-north-east of the country, which largely coincided with the regions where the city-republics flourished in the medieval period) and the German Baden-Württemberg. A leading theorist of the post-Fordist economies of flexible specialization has been Michael Storper, an economic geographer who has played a central role in the institutionalist understanding of endogenous local development. In the 1990s, Storper concentrated his attention on the resurgence of regional economies, theorizing the ways in which successful regions are those capable of mobilizing what he called 'untraded interdependences': a diversified set of socio-cultural factors contributing in varying degrees to the regional pathways of economic specialization, such as face-to-face contact, tacit knowledge, efficient institutions and social networks (Storper, 1995). Along related lines, Ash Amin and Nigel Thrift coined the influential notion of 'institutional thickness', which was intended to make sense of the tremendous variety of formal and informal institutions, conventions, and modes of social interaction at the heart of the rise of post-Fordist regions (Amin and Thrift, 1995). The same phenomenon was understood by Philip Cooke and Kevin Morgan in terms of 'economies of association', a notion emphasizing the fact that a rich repertoire of intermediary institutions facilitates interaction amongst local actors in a market-led economy (Cooke and Morgan, 1999).

In recent times, Michael Storper has expanded his institutionalist understanding of local economic development, looking at successful city-regions, particularly those capable of embracing technology-intensive economic growth pathways. In his view, communities and social groups provide an essential contribution to the institutional base, as understood above, of cities and city-regions (Storper, 2013). However, as Storper points out, an interpretation of local economic development based only on the act of bonding to place-based communities, which characterized the regional development scholarship dealing with flexible specialization in the 1990s, offers a limited understanding of the contemporary dynamics of urban and regional development. Bonding and the sense of place-based belonging are important, but also processes and acts of 'bridging' between and across different groups are vital to the competitiveness of contemporary city-regions. In Storper's view, this means overcoming the customary community–society dualism which has long dominated social theory, starting with the famous Tönnies-Weber's discussion around the distinction between *Gemeinschaft* (community), associated with pre-modern social relations, and *Gesellschaft* (society), tied to capitalist structures of rationality. According to Storper, the act of 'bridging' is associated with the idea of society: its translation into the political sphere leads to the formation of pro-growth coalitions (or developmental coalitions, in his words). While recognizing the fact that coalitions are 'essential to development because they provide a context in which good ideas and policies can be implemented' (Storper, 2013: 119), he leaves this issue unexplored, not engaging with the large urban scholarship that from the 1980s onwards has investigated the rise and proliferation of pro-growth coalitions, entrepreneurial cities and public–private partnerships within the urban political landscape at a time of globalization and increasingly heightened inter-city competition (Hall and Hubbard, 1998).

Within this urban scholarship, the phenomenon of urban entrepreneurialism has been interpreted mainly as a consequence of structural shifts occurring in the dominant mode of regulation in contemporary capitalist societies, namely the dismissal of Keynesian distributional approaches to societal government and the embrace of neoliberal, growth-first governmental rationalities (Harvey, 1989b). In the 1980s, amidst the post-Fordist transition, therefore, the field of urban studies became concerned with the rise of pro-growth urban regimes. This led to a focus on the local scale of interaction: from the amenity-led revitalization of downtowns and waterfronts, to urban regeneration processes at the neighbourhood level and, in ex-industrial areas, based on the renewal of the housing supply and the reconversion of previous manufacturing spaces into post-industrial sites. This literature was particularly rooted in the fields of political science (studies on urban regimes) and sociology (source of the idea of growth coalitions: Logan and Molotch, 1987). From the 1990s onwards, critical urban scholars particularly in human geography began showing their dissatisfaction with the localistic bias of previous scholarship. In doing so, they concentrated their attention on the multiple geographical scales of urban entrepreneurialism, starting from the dialectic between the global and the local, particularly within the framework of the so-called re-scaling of urban governance (Swyngedouw, 1992; Brenner, 1999).

In the last ten or fifteen years, however, even the multiscalar approach has appeared to limit the heuristic potential of urban studies, and a larger set of socio-spatial relations involved in processes of urban entrepreneurialism has thus emerged. In a context of increasingly multicentric globalization, urban politico-economic elites look for larger but also more flexible and dynamic coalitions and actor-networks. In a recent study, David Wachsmuth has called attention to the rise of phenomena of unstable coalition formation and 'post-city politics' in the US context (Wachsmuth, 2014; see also Rickards et al., 2016). Ideas of planetary urbanization and global urbanism have gained wide currency in recent years, providing an explanation of the United Nations' urban age thesis that goes beyond the demographic variable and 'provincializing' what appears to be a persistently West-centric urban scholarship, respectively (Brenner and Schmid, 2014; Sheppard et al., 2013). While some authors fear a loss of the idea of the city itself within these interpretive frameworks (Scott and Storper, 2015), there is no doubt that urban politics and the city–capitalism nexus should be rethought in light of the ongoing processes of extended urbanization of the planet (see chapter 2).

In particular, we can understand the geographical extension of urban politics beyond the local scale and the local–global dichotomy indeed emanates from the growing intertwinedness of cities and capitalism in the global age. A key entry point for the study of this linkage remains the notion of urban entrepreneurialism, which has become a distinguishing feature of neoliberal societies in times of globalization. What the literature on urban entrepreneurialism shows is the way in which economic growth acts as a bridging force – to put it in Storper's institutionalist terms – between different sets of political, economic and spatial entities. Against this conceptual backdrop, one can identify three stages within the evolutionary path of contemporary urban entrepreneurialism.

First, the original phenomenon of contemporary city entrepreneurialism took shape during the early stages of the process of contemporary globalization and the concomitant neoliberalization of urban environments from the late 1970s onwards. In this context, what is defined as the 'bridging process' involved public and private actors and related organizations aiming to reconvert land uses and revalorize urban spaces, after the decline of Fordism and the related pattern of urbanization. This foundational urban entrepreneurialism concentrated essentially on the local scale of interaction and, from a neoliberal perspective, it was essential for getting rid of the Keynesian legacy, in terms of welfare-state institutions reminiscent of that allegedly 'failed' mode of regulation. This objective was achieved through processes of privatization of public services and the managerialization of governance structures, as well as the delegitimization of issues of redistribution as a key concern for public policy. Urban societies had to become accustomed to an entirely new vocabulary, deeply imbued with neoliberal values of competition and privatism, civic boosterism and individual responsibilization, within a general conception of the city as a growth-oriented machine. In this phase, the bonding dimension of urban politics was still decisive to the pursuit of cohesive pro-growth coalitions. The resultant neoliberal rationality of urban management relied primarily on the renewed sense of belonging to urban communities and the willingness to engage in public–private partnerships. The numerous processes of coalition-making that characterized the neoliberal politics of urban development in the 1980s were therefore intended to build a bridge between different communities mobilizing for urban and economic regeneration after the economic shock of the first half of the 1970s that led to an era of deindustrialization and urban decline.

Second, from the early 1990s onwards, the idea of globalization became explicit and increasingly predominant within public discourse. While in previous years its use was still confined to narrow circles of specialists such as academic scholars and business consultants, at this time globalization suddenly became the new catchword within public debates and even the popular mass media. Observers of different political-ideological orientation pointed to the inadequacies of the nation-state and its disempowerment, predicting the advent of a 'borderless world' (Ohmae, 1990) or, more realistically, scrutinizing the so-called 'hollowing out' of the nation-state (Jessop, 1994). In a context characterized by the alleged demise of the centrality of the nation-state and the rise of the global city phenomenon, cities started engaging in what urban scholars defined 'the local politics of globalization' (Cochrane et al., 1996): municipal authorities with the support of rent-seeking local actors realized that the key to urban resurgence was the capacity to build bridges between cities and international organizations and investors, obtaining the designation of mega-events and attracting the interest of global brands. Europe provided illustrative evidence of this stage of urban entrepreneurialism: the rapid ascent of Barcelona as an emerging leading city after its Olympic designation; the renaissance of Bilbao and the so-called Guggenheimization of urban development; the material reorganization and the symbolic reimagination of Berlin after the German unification are well-known examples in this respect.

Third, in the last fifteen years, with the rise of a more multipolar world and the increased circulation of urban policies and development models, cities have ramified their networks, alliances and coalitions, with the involvement of a broader array of public and private institutions, international organizations and economic players. Mega-events and global brands obviously still attract the interest of politico-economic decision-makers across the world, particularly in the emerging economies of the global South, but also in the peripheries of the global North. The new developmentalist impetus in the global South has induced the Brazilian government to bid successfully for the two biggest sports events – the Football World Cup of 2014 and the Summer Olympics of 2016 – at a time in which Brazil was seen as an emerging economic superpower, particularly after the discovery of a large oil field in 2006. During the same period, in the quieter context of Northern Europe, Finland was in search of a new attractive image after losing its reputation as the telecommunications world centre with the decline of Nokia: the opening of a local branch of the internationally renowned Guggenheim museum in Helsinki was regarded as an ideal solution (see chapter 4).

However, politico-economic elites are increasingly cognizant that these major designations are attractive opportunities for local economic development, but are also likely to turn quickly into highly controversial projects, being seen as easy short cuts for a promised prosperity. In Brazil, the first warning was in 2013 when angry youths took to the streets to protest against the waste of public money for the Football World Cup (see also chapter 5); in Helsinki, over the years the local arts and design community has become increasingly averse to the Guggenheim project, whose finalization has been openly disputed (Volner, 2015; see chapter 4). The example of Athens being an apparently successful Olympic city in 2004, then hit by an unprecedented austerity programme only a few years later, acts as a spectre of an urban entrepreneurialism predicated on mega-events. In Brazil, the recent sport mega-events have coincided with a precipitous economic slowdown (in 2010 GDP growth was at +7 per cent; five years later at the end of 2015 it was down to −6 per cent) and an unprecedented crisis of legitimacy for the ruling political class that has culminated in an impeachment process against President Dilma Rousseff, started in December 2015.

These examples show a crisis of the mega-event or the mega-project understood as 'environments of enclosure' in Foucault's terms (the urban version of disciplinary institutions like prison, factory, hospital and school), being used by governing elites as a way of imposing a disciplinary regime on urban societies in the name of economic development and urban renaissance: as Gilles Deleuze argued, the crisis of disciplinary society paves the way to the advent of a society of control where dispersal replaces concentration (Deleuze, 1992). Michael Hardt and Antonio Negri have reinterpreted Deleuze's idea of the shift from a disciplinary society to a society of control against the backdrop of their theorization of the real subsumption of society in the post-Fordist state, where the 'logic of capitalist production perfected in the factory now invests all forms of social production equally' (Hardt and Negri, 1994: 259).

At the city level, one can observe this shift in the way in which city managers and policymakers increasingly engage in relational processes involving a wider set of actors, institutions and funding sources coalescing around globally hegemonic urban development models. The proliferation and rapid turnover of policy catchwords and corresponding urban development imperatives is revelatory of this socialized regime of urban control: in response to the crisis of disciplinary mechanisms of urban development, such as the mega-event and the mega-project, today's cities are demanded to be at one and the same time smart, start-up-friendly, resilient and creative. This overwhelming panoply of imperatives and imaginaries increases the complexity of the city–capitalism nexus, witnessing an intensified circulation of economic development models and alleged best practices (Peck and Theodore, 2015), but also a multifaceted process of social bonding and bridging involving different communities and spatialities. According to influential authors in contemporary urban and regional scholarship, these developments urge us to go beyond the one-dimensionalism of socio-spatial relations characterizing both place-centred and scalar understandings of urban and regional processes: in their view, contemporary strategies of urban and regional development are to be viewed as a combination, sometimes overlapping, sometimes alternating, of structuration processes centred on different spatialities and socio-spatial relations, in which those based on ideas of territory, place, scale and networks seem to be prevalent (Jessop et al., 2008).

The three stages of urban entrepreneurialism outlined in this section have thus showed the evolutionary path of cities in their relationship to capitalism in the contemporary context of neoliberalism and globalization over the last four decades or so. In the early stages of neoliberalism, capitalist cities saw the rise of the entrepreneurialization of urban governance, through the alliance between public and private actors within pro-growth coalitions. Subsequently, with the rise of globalization as a dominant discourse and representation of the world economy, this competitive terrain was rearranged within the hierarchical architectures of multiscalar governance. Finally, the emerging context of increasingly multicentric globalization has prepared the ground for cities and regions to get rid of the previous dominance of rigidly hierarchical governance arrangements. This enables them to mobilize what Bob Jessop has more recently defined 'multi-spatial meta-governance', particularly in the context of the global economic crisis and the subsequent post-recession transition (Jessop, 2016): the institutional capacity to deal with different spatialities and corresponding imaginaries of capitalist growth. City entrepreneurialism, therefore, originally came out of the spatially bounded phenomenon of municipal civicness in the Italian city-republics of the Middle Ages, as analysed by Putnam, and has ended up becoming a polymorphous engine of urban globalization within the context of contemporary global capitalism.

COGNITIVE CAPITAL

In *Cities in Civilization*, a monumental book dedicated to reconstructing the historical trajectory of contemporary cities, geographer and urban planner Peter Hall brought together the great cultural, economic-technological and organizational innovations associated with the urban phenomenon in the long run since its appearance in human history (Hall, 1998). The book was published in the late 1990s at a time when social scientists were coming to grips with the revolutionary consequences of what Manuel Castells had defined 'the network society', characterized by the eruption of information technologies within capitalist economies and societies (Castells, 1989 and 1996). The use of information technologies soon appeared to be 'revolutionary', as it transgressed established boundaries within both economic sectors and established business practices. Peter Hall's aim was to look at the present age of information society in a long-term perspective, viewing the force of technological innovation as a driver of contemporary transformations of both capitalism and urbanization. To do so, he showed how the different phases of pre-industrial, industrial and post-industrial capitalism have been intimately associated with paradigmatic cities, but he also went beyond the mere association of cities with technological innovation under mature capitalism, looking at the urban encounter of art, culture, technology and organization as the quintessential feature of Western civilization and its 'continued vitality' from the classic age onwards (Hall, 1998).

Peter Hall's distinctive contribution has been his extra-economic (or to put it another way: 'more-than-economic') understanding of the role of cities in human civilization, particularly the ways in which cities have acted as heterogeneous agglomerations of different forms of knowledge, information and intellectual skills. In this perspective, the age of industrial capitalism has to be viewed as just one phase within a long-term trajectory that has led cities to establish themselves as complex sites of knowledge accumulation. In conceptual terms, in his book Peter Hall has drawn on what at that time was still a peripheral strand of theorization: what he called the 'theories of the creative city', notably Gunnar Törnqvist's theorization of the 'creative milieu' as the outcome of four activities, which first appeared in the late 1970s: information exchanges, knowledge accumulation, instrumental competences, and creativity, a systemic feature that stems from the combination of the previous three (see Törnqvist, 2011).

In economic history and the wider social sciences, capitalism's perpetual search for economic and technological innovation has been customarily linked to Joseph Schumpeter's theory of the business cycles and the innovative entrepreneur, particularly his famous creative-destruction metaphor (Schumpeter, 1939). In the 1990s, along with Peter Hall, the rise of cities and regions as places of innovation and capitalist resurgence attracted the interest of urban economists offering a place-based reinterpretation of Schumpeter, coining the notion of 'innovative milieu' (or *milieu innovateur*: Camagni, 1995). In more recent years, increasingly influential strands of research at the intersection between economic geography and applied economics, such as evolutionary economics and knowledge management studies, have illuminated the environmental and spatial dimensions of technological innovation, building on the pioneering research of economists who looked at phenomena of information flows and knowledge spillovers within agglomeration economies in the study of high-tech regional industrial clusters (Audretsch and Feldman, 1996). The emphasis laid on innovation and the production of knowledge as social processes, therefore, has not remained confined to heterodox circles of economic historians, human geographers and urban and regional planners. In the latter a pioneering role was played in the 1980s by critical urbanists, who were concerned with the investigation of post-Fordist economies, originally inspired by Marxist political economy, and who examined the increasing role acquired by knowledge within contemporary capitalism, as well as the central role played by cities in this context, paying stronger attention to the institutional context and the socio-spatial implications behind technology-intensive capital accumulation.

A key reference in this respect is the work by Allen Scott, who began with the analysis of technological production complexes in California in the 1980s, then focused on the cultural economy in Los Angeles in the 1990s, eventually dealing with the urban manifestation of what he calls 'cognitive-cultural capitalism': a set of socio-economically differentiated knowledge-intensive economies emerging in a context marked by the rise of city-regions as political actors (Scott, 2008 and 2014). In recent times, along with Michael Storper, Scott has dedicated his critical endeavours to uncovering the limitations of the dominant theories of creative and smart urbanism, of which Richard Florida (2012), Edward Glaeser (2011) and Enrico Moretti (2012) are influential proponents within scholarly and public debates alike. These authors and the large body of literature following their approaches build on the fundamental assumption that 'jobs follow places' in today's highly mobile societies, and that the task of city governments is to improve the living conditions of their cities through investment in amenities (Glaeser's position), through the relaxation of environmental rules and zoning regulations constraining the housing market, which currently afflict the mobility of high-skilled workers (Moretti's position), and through the enhancement of the cultural attractiveness of the urban environment, satisfying the 'post-materialist' needs of the members of the creative class (Florida's thesis). (See also chapter 3 for further discussion.)

Storper and Scott criticize this approach, based on the idea that the decisive factor in urban development pathways consists in the preferences of the individual consumer or worker, arguing instead that the path-dependent logic of production, agglomeration and regional specialization is a key determinant of processes of economic growth and urban revitalization (Storper and Scott, 2009).

Albeit differentiated in many respects, in their work Peter Hall, Manuel Castells and Allen Scott have offered similar understandings of the socio-institutional bases of technology-led urban and regional development. They consider that cities' engagement with technology and processes of innovation should be viewed as the outcome of trajectories of urban economic development and the mobilization of a complex set of actors and economic drivers, such as universities and other research institutions acting as incubators for innovative businesses, the uneven supply of venture capital and the role of local governments, as well as intangible factors such as a culture of risk and entrepreneurship. At the same time, these authors also agree that the advent of the network and information society – as defined by Manuel Castells – has radically transformed urban economies, producing something radically new in capitalist history. While these authors have aptly explored the institutional configuration of present-day knowledge-intensive forms of capitalism, post-structuralist theorists of cognitive capitalism have called attention to the larger valorization of human life within the changing dynamics of capital accumulation. In a sense, it can be argued that they have offered a theorization of post-Fordist capitalism as a materialization of Peter Hall's idea of cities as innovative entities transgressing the boundaries between economy, culture and society. In this perspective, processes of capitalist innovation are no longer circumscribed to the firm, the research laboratory or to being merely the product of state-led economic development policy, as was the case for the rise of post-war high-tech complexes in the US Sunbelt (see chapter 4). In particular, Michael Hardt and

Antonio Negri have understood contemporary processes of informatization of production as a shift from the formal subsumption of labour under capital prevailing in industrial capitalism, to the 'real subsumption' of society and life itself, which entails the capitalist valorization of knowledge, affects and relational abilities – what Marx called 'the general intellect' in his visionary 'fragment on machines' text (Hardt and Negri, 2000; see chapter 5). In a similar vein, geographer Nigel Thrift has offered a theorization of what he calls 'economies of invention' centred on the capitalist commodification of the 'whole intellect', through cultural mechanisms that involve the everyday dimension of economic activity: from marketing strategies to business consultancy and training forums (Thrift, 2005).

In order to understand cognitive capitalism and its urban dimension, it is worth paying greater attention to the work of Hardt and Negri, which has been particularly influential in larger political and intellectual debates, but has been overlooked in urban studies and the other socio-spatial sciences. While in *Empire* Hardt and Negri showed little interest in local and regional scales, in *Commonwealth* (the third book of their trilogy on capitalism and globalization) they explicitly refer to the metropolis as the privileged site of biopolitical production in contemporary societies, generating forms of life that add value to knowledge-intensive capitalism (Hardt and Negri, 2009). In their analysis, Hardt and Negri interestingly take the example of real estate as a key sector in contemporary capitalist societies, emphasizing the extractive power of what they call 'externalities'; namely, what landowners and real-estate agents see as the positive aspects of location increasing the exchange value of the built environment. On the other hand, what is seen as a negative externality is promptly removed from the urban landscape. The logic of extraction is thus systematically accompanied by that of expulsion, particularly affecting undesirable groups and populations (Sassen, 2014). In valorizing the externalities of urban settings, Hardt and Negri contend, real-estate developers appropriate the common wealth generated by the metropolis. Looking through the lens of Hart and Negri's framework at Florida and Glaeser's theorizations of creative and consumer-oriented urbanism, stressing the 'quality of place' and the role of amenities, we can therefore discern their intent to provide supporting evidence and theoretical justification for the capitalist process of appropriation of the urban 'commonwealth'.

Today, this process of extraction involves a tremendous variety of urban spaces. On the one hand, leading urban theorists like Richard Florida emphasize the 'urban shift' in the geography of venture capital, looking at the way in which a new generation of high-tech start-up enterprises has proliferated within inner-city districts across the USA and other countries in the world (Florida, 2014). In the US context, this phenomenon is now known as the tech boom 2.0, as it comes after the first boom of Internet-based technology companies in the late 1990s, which was disrupted by the bursting of the dot-com bubble in 2000–1. The recent tech boom particularly exploits the communicative potential offered by online social media and networks in different ways: professional entrepreneurs give rise to dialogic communities of practice, conveying a sense of the entrepreneurial activity as an experience of social cooperation; consumers become involved in the process of creation and redesign of goods through artifices like the so-called 'user-generated content'; and ordinary people reinvent themselves as part-time entrepreneurs through their involvement in the technology-based sharing economy. As this book will show, technology is no longer just a niche but is now at the centre of contemporary pathways of urban economic regeneration and is also behind their contradictions, which include the rise of new socio-spatial inequalities that are linked to overheated housing markets in super-gentrified cities. This phenomenon takes place within a context of post-recession transition (following the 'great contraction' of the late 2000s), characterized by an increasingly turbulent global economy and by slow-growth rates, thus acting as an anti-depressant to reawaken the dormant 'animal spirits of capitalism'.

The start-up phenomenon is truly global, involving cities in the most disparate corners of the world: it powerfully shows how the entrepreneurial culture of capitalism has expanded, while urban environments act as magnets for technology businesses and a stratified experience economy which transgresses the boundaries of the formalized firm, involving potentially all urban dwellers and their everyday lives.

In this context, in the emerging economies of the global South, deeply marginalized spaces such as the slums in India and the favelas in Brazil are increasingly attracting the interest not only of real-estate developers, eager to turn slum dwellers into a new class of homeowners and consumers (Mukhija, 2003), but also of the most powerful high-tech corporations in the contemporary global economy. As *The Wall Street Journal* enthusiastically reports, in Rio de Janeiro, Brazil, both Microsoft and Google have recently launched campaigns involving local residents, who use their smartphones to map the informal settlements of the favelas that are customarily excluded from official maps, with an emphasis on the locations of existing businesses within these spaces (Connors, 2014). While the *WSJ* article points to the commercial potential of the favelas in terms of consumption and business-generation opportunities, these initiatives have far more ambitious goals. Microsoft and Google are examples of what Nicole Aschoff has recently defined the 'new prophets of capital' and the associated phenomenon of 'philanthropicapitalism': unlike the old capitalists engaging in conventional charity initiatives, these visionary capitalists – directly or through dedicated foundations – embody a new generation of 'elite storytellers' promoting 'solutions to society's problems that can be found within the logic of existing profit-driven structures of production and consumption' and, in doing so, they 'reinforce the logic and structure of accumulation' (Aschoff, 2015: 11–12). Along with a wide array of economic and cultural players such as NGOs, policy consultants, artists and creative entrepreneurs, these 'prophets of capital' are protagonists of what Ananya Roy has evocatively described as 'slumdog urbanism' (Roy, 2011), where the subalternity of the urban condition is subsumed within the imaginary of contemporary capitalism and progressively within the material mechanisms of its incessantly expanding value chain, pointing to consumption, homeownership and entrepreneurial spirit as the foundations of a new era of social well-being.

In this context, multinational corporations, the mass media and government leaders, but also civil-society organizations and local residents, variously contribute to the propagation of values, lifestyles and techniques (such as microfinance) that co-produce the fantasy of the 'entrepreneurial slum', where poverty is seen as a capital and the poor as creative entrepreneurs (McFarlane, 2012). Within advanced post-Fordist societies, therefore, the cognitive capital of contemporary cities includes but also goes beyond the professional producers of knowledge and innovation, customarily identified within economic and urban scholarship as the so-called 'creative class', 'consumer city' and 'smart labour'. The future of global capitalism depends on the ways in which these multifaceted components of cognitive capital will be brought together and the inherent contradictions in this process of assemblage will be dealt with in public policy.

CONCLUSION

This chapter has provided the starting point for the analysis of today's association of cities with global capitalism that will be developed in greater detail in the rest of this book. The aim of this chapter has not been to provide a conventionally historical overview of the city–capitalism nexus. On the contrary, the proposed reconstruction has been intentionally selective, identifying long-term features of the urban phenomenon that appear not only to have survived throughout centuries of human history but also to have become essential for the current stage of global capitalist urbanization: financial power, entrepreneurialism and cognitive capital. In a Foucauldian sense, this chapter offers 'a history of the present' (Foucault, 1995: 31), showing how – as Benedetto Croce's famous dictum puts it – 'every true history is contemporary history' (Croce, 1921: 13). The intentionally 'presentist' approach used in this chapter and throughout the book helps us identify the historical emergences of urban capitalist societies – what has come to the surface from long-term as well as short-term processes of selection and retention, becoming increasingly more visible, effective and socio-spatially pervasive.

In other words, the fact that contemporary capitalist cities rely heavily on financial power, entrepreneurialism and cognitive capital does not take place in a vacuum, but is the outcome of pre-existing emergences, which the current era of neoliberalism and globalization has revived and expanded both socially and spatially. This claim is not intended to reiterate the path-dependency argument, which is nowadays influential within the social sciences, with its linear conception of socio-economic processes in which social facts appear to be determined by history in the last instance. While the long-term key forces nurturing the city–capitalism nexus over the centuries have laid the foundations for the current 'urban age', the final chapter and the conclusion of this book will be dedicated to analysing the 'present as history', emphasizing the indeterminacy (the 'ambivalence') of societal transformations and the clarifying function of politics.

2 | Extensions ————————————————————

LOOKING FOR THE GLOBAL

In the previous chapter it was particularly emphasized how the advent of globalization has reasserted the centrality of cities, with their growing involvement in capitalism as the dominant mode of production and economic development strategy in the contemporary world. Cities have played a central role, both in the early stages of primordial capitalism, preceding the formation of the modern nation-state and the Industrial Revolution, and later, when weakening nation-states had renegotiated their positionality in the context of increasingly complex, multiscalar, governance arrangements within the contemporary world economy (Brenner, 2004). Since its appearance within public and scholarly debates, the idea of globalization has been intimately associated with the urban phenomenon. Thanks to the work of Saskia Sassen, in particular, world cities like London, Tokyo and New York came to symbolize the novel scenario of capitalist globalization, as concentrations at one and the same time of financial institutions, ethnic diversity and socio-spatial inequalities.

Today, the renewed centrality of cities is stressed by social scientists not only in economic terms, but also in a political vein. In a book provocatively entitled *If Mayors Ruled the World*, US political scientist Benjamin Barber contends that city governments are the only credible alternative to increasingly paralyzed nation-states, as customary mechanisms of cooperation and decision-making allow cities to act in increasingly coordinated ways to address a growing number of societal issues, many of which – such as trade, climate change, public health, immigration and technology – exceed the traditional sphere of urban government (Barber, 2013; see also Katz and Bradley, 2013). This claim is not new, but it has accompanied the rise of globalization since its inception. Previous debates in the 1990s and the early 2000s about global cities and the emerging sense of urban citizenship, for example, emphasized the role of cities as a potential 'homebase for cosmopolitan democracy' (Bauböck, 2003). From this perspective, it was argued that cities should be granted autonomy from nation-states in terms of membership and rights, as well as on issues for which nation-states have so far retained their monopoly power, such as trade, immigration and foreign policy.

This chapter will not engage specifically with the thesis of cities as global political actors, as this largely normative assumption does not take into account actually existing power relationships in the world economy, namely the fact that nation-states are still powerful political entities exerting decisive influence over domestic affairs and global diplomacy. However, at the same time, there is no doubt that both the economic centrality acquired by cities and the evident failures of nation-states in coping with issues like immigration and foreign policy make these claims reasonable and realistic. The aim of this chapter is to explore the evolving role played by cities as interconnecting spatialities between globalization and capitalism, as understood within urban scholarship. Moreover, elaborating on the interpretive framework constructed in chapter 1, this chapter will show how the association of cities with capitalism has become more pervasive in both geographical and societal terms at a time of advanced globalization, in a context of so-called planetary urbanization and global urbanism. Urban scholars, particularly those specializing in the global South who are conceptually inspired by postcolonial theories, have rightly emphasized the need to go beyond the West-centric views still predominant within existing urban scholarship, inviting us to look at the urban phenomenon from a truly global perspective. However, what this literature has not yet done is to illuminate the role played by capitalism as the driving force behind global urbanization and urbanism. Scholars putting forward the thesis of planetary urbanization do not neglect the role of capitalism, but they look at capitalism essentially as a disaggregating and coercive force, destabilizing previous spatial orders and imposing new spatial arrangements in which urban and newly urbanized environments become crucial. While recognizing the relevance of these interpretations, this book also calls attention to the surplus value generated by cities within the cultural logic of communicative-cognitive capitalism in a context of advanced globalization. In particular, this chapter looks at the ways in which the renewed interconnectedness of globalization, capitalism and urbanism is illustrative not just of the expansion of urbanization in the contemporary world, as the planetary urbanization thesis puts it, but also of the economic valorization of cities and their societies. Against this background, the chapter examines the evolution of studies and debates around cities and globalization within contemporary urban scholarship, showing how this reflects a more expanded view of capitalism in its urban manifestation while arguing for an extension of our understanding of the city–capitalism nexus in times of advanced globalization.

Here, six main steps are identified in the evolutionary trajectory of scholarship dealing with the capitalist globalization of the urban phenomenon, from the territorial and structuralist views of John Friedmann, Saskia Sassen and Peter Taylor in the 1980s and the 1990s to subsequent accounts centred on ideas of world city-network, transnationalism and relational processes of urban globalization. The chapter concludes with a critical review of the recent debate over the planetary urbanization thesis.

STRUCTURING CAPITALIST GLOBALIZATION

Since the early 1980s, social sciences witnessed increasing attention dedicated to the role played by cities within the world economy. At that time, the concomitant crises of Fordism and Keynesianism, along with the popularity acquired by the so-called world-system analysis within the critical social sciences, led to studies investigating the changing division of labour within the international economy and how cities and regions contribute to the emerging context and the related dynamics of capital accumulation. The second half of the 1980s saw the so-called 'global shift' within the world economy, as social scientists and the public alike became aware of the advent of globalization and started theorizing it in explicit ways (Dicken, 1986). In this process of discovery of globalization as a key phenomenon of the post-Cold War era, initially confined to the industrial sphere as in Peter Dicken's account, cities acquired an increasingly prominent role as strongholds of economic power and knowledge production. The 'territorial' view of the city-globalization relationship predominant in the 1990s, looking at cities as circumscribed geographical entities concentrating spatially fixed economic functions and structures (McCann and Ward, 2010), was later questioned by authors looking at inter-city relationships through the lenses of transnational urban networks, which were observed both 'from above' (at the level of global corporations) and 'from below' (at the level of transnational immigrant communities).

The world-city hypothesis

Early scholarship looking at cities from the perspective of the world economy prioritized research on the functional endowments allowing cities to act as engines of the contemporary process of globalization. Two key structural shifts resulted from the crisis of Fordist-Keynesian capitalism in the 1970s: first, the transition towards a new international division of labour on a global scale, as a consequence of delocalization processes from the Western countries to the 'less-developed' economies in the South and other peripheral regions of the world; second, the shift towards a service-centred economy within advanced capitalist countries. These structural processes had two consequences for cities understood as economic spaces. On the one hand, to varying degrees cities acquired the role of providers of knowledge-intensive business services, such urban agglomerations being labelled 'global cities'; on the other hand, the new international division of labour paved the way for the emergence of global commodity chains, which required the development of logistical functions and spaces where finished or semi-finished products could circulate across the globe. This led to so-called 'gateway cities', namely, cities acting as hubs with their seaports and airports specializing in the supply of these services (Short et al., 2000). In the new international division of labour, therefore, cities played a key role as regards both intangible and tangible factors crucial to the functioning of the global economy.

Against this backdrop, urban planner John Friedmann and other scholars started looking particularly at world cities in the context of the changing international division of labour (Friedmann and Wolf, 1982). Even though the precursors of world-city research had limited their study of globalization to the economic sphere (Smith and Feagin, 1987), seemingly unaware of globalization as a discursive process that forged institutional practices and capital accumulation strategies, Friedmann and his colleagues (including Saskia Sassen) were committed to investigating phenomena of growing interdependence between central and peripheral regions in the world economy. As such, these were seen from the standpoint of the increasingly greater influence exerted by multinational corporations over the general economic activity (Friedmann, 1986). Since the late 1960s, when he published a monograph dealing with regional development policy in Venezuela,

Friedmann had been a key proponent of the thesis concerning unequal exchange between centre and periphery, the former specializing in technology-based sectors and the latter in low-value, mainly agricultural production (Friedmann, 1966). His study provided evidence of the regional implications of the dynamics of uneven geographical development, which at that time attracted the interest of neo-Marxist economists in the third world, such as Andre Gunder Frank and Samir Amin, amongst others.

Moreover, Friedmann's subsequent work on world-city formation drew inspiration from Immanuel Wallerstein's world-systems analysis, theorizing the world economy as a system based on relations of dominance and subordination, whose features are determined by historical cycles of capital accumulation (Wallerstein, 1979). When he formulated the world-city hypothesis, Friedmann identified a 'world system of cities', within which there is a narrow circle of urban centres which for historical reasons hold a hegemonic position, controlling from a distance the integrated functioning of the international economy, by hosting the headquarters of multinational firms and international organizations. In particular, he proposed a 'hierarchy' of world cities, distinguishing between those located in the 'core countries' – the industrialized, market-led economies – and those located in the semi-peripheral countries, namely middle-income nations which had completed their transition towards a market-based economy. At the top of the former, Friedmann identified London in Western Europe, New York in North America and Tokyo in Asia, while at the top of the latter there were São Paulo, Singapore and Hong Kong. Even though his theses lacked a clear empirical base, Friedmann's work had the merit of laying the foundations of a research programme destined to be path-breaking, not only within urban and regional studies but also in the wider social sciences and public debates. Through such steps, a novel understanding of the relationship linking cities, capitalism and the global economy was developed within urban scholarship and the social sciences.

The global-city thesis

Friedmann's pioneering theses found a particularly fertile ground in the emerging discourse around globalization. And a decisive contribution to the increased awareness of the directional role and the related command functions acquired by cities within the globalizing economy came from Saskia Sassen, an economic and urban sociologist who had previously collaborated with John Friedmann. While acknowledging the importance of Friedmann's foundational writings, Sassen underlined the novelty represented by 'the fact of globalization' as a crucial determinant of the capitalist economy and the urban phenomenon, not only in economic-financial terms but also in terms of socio-spatial organization. In doing so, Sassen drew attention to two essential manifestations of the new stage of capitalist development and the related global-city phenomenon: the dynamics of socio-polarization and the attraction of advanced producer services (Sassen, 1994). At the time of her collaboration with John Friedmann, Sassen had already analysed the process of restructuring in New York following the crisis of the mid-1970s, putting forward the idea that the transition towards a service-oriented economy leads to a dynamic of socio-spatial polarization. On the one hand, there is the attraction of high-income professionals holding top-level positions within the business services; on the other hand, the economic valorization of urban spaces – as a consequence of the concentration of multinational corporations' headquarters and a wide range of producer services – stimulates the growth of labour-intensive services for both businesses and consumers (from building maintenance and cleaning services to manual labour in shops and restaurants), which is characterized by low wages. The latter services become occupational niches for unskilled international migrants as well as for the residual indigenous workforce. This process of socio-spatial polarization is reflected at the residential level, with the spread of gentrification processes in newly regenerated neighbourhoods juxtaposed with the concomitant segregation of low-income ethnic minorities in deprived areas on the outskirts and in physically decaying inner-city districts (Sassen-Koob, 1986).

In subsequent years, Saskia Sassen systematized her theses, concentrating on the triad of global cities that held a hegemonic position within the world economy – London, New York and Tokyo – and focusing on the role played by producer services as determinants of global-city rank. In particular, Sassen identified a geography of centralities and marginalities at different geographical scales. On the one hand, at the inter-urban scale, the dialectic between centrality and marginality was exemplified by the hegemonic position held by some cities (for example, Paris, Frankfurt, Zurich, Amsterdam, Los Angeles, Sydney and Hong Kong) and the growing marginality of cities that had experienced processes of economic decline (like old manufacturing and port cities: Turin and Liverpool in Western Europe, Philadelphia and Detroit in the USA). On the other hand, at the intra-urban scale, the centrality–marginality dialectic was illustrated by the divide between regenerating neighbourhoods and marginalized areas, which were excluded from state-led revitalization programmes as well as capital investment in the built environment (Sassen, 1994).

In the final analysis, Sassen's work is recognized for the emphasis she has placed on producer services and the related processes of dominance and peripherality within the world economy, while in previous literature dealing with world-city formation the emphasis was on world cities as favourite locations for the headquarters of multinational corporations.

The network-centred perspective

Although the emerging global-city scholarship in the 1990s produced substantial advancement in both theoretical-methodological and empirical terms compared with the studies of the previous decade, there was still a lack of systematic enquiry regarding the hierarchical stratification of world cities within the global economy. The Globalization and World Cities (GaWC) research network, led by geographer Peter Taylor at the University of Loughborough in the UK, filled this void by offering a detailed ranking of world cities in relation to producer services, thus providing a more solid empirical base to Saskia Sassen's interpretive framework:

> taking our cue from Sassen (1991, p. 126), we treat world cities as particular 'postindustrial production sites' where innovations in corporate services and finance have been integral to the recent restructuring of the world economy now widely known as globalization. (Beaverstock et al., 1999: 450)

In particular, the GaWC research network provided a statistically accurate analysis of producer services in four key sectors (insurance, advertising, banking and law), ranking 122 cities on the basis of their positionality on the world scale. Of the ten cities placed at the top of the ranking, four were found in Western Europe (London, Paris, Frankfurt, Milan), three in North America (New York, Chicago, Los Angeles) and three in East Asia (Tokyo, Hong Kong, Singapore). Among the top ten, London, Paris, New York and Tokyo obtained the highest ranking, thus confirming Friedmann and Sassen's previous identifications of a triad of global cities, with the addition of Paris.

It is striking to observe the relative stability of world-city rankings over time, despite the strong turbulence that has hit the global economy in recent years. In the ranking published by GaWC in 2012, what is noticeable is the ascendancy of key cities in the so-called BRICS countries and in emerging economies in the Middle East, such as Mumbai (in which in 1999 researchers found only an evidence of 'world-city formation'), Shanghai, Beijing and Dubai (see: <http://

www.lboro.ac.uk/gawc/world2012t.html>). However, leading positions are still firmly held by established global cities such as New York and London, despite these cities being at the centre of the economic turmoil caused by the financial crash of 2008.

In conceptual and methodological terms, researchers of the GaWC have not limited their contribution to the provision of more systematic empirical evidence for Sassen's thesis of global cities. Their work has added an important innovation to this scholarship: the invitation to look not only at the position of each city within the world-city rankings but also to observe the inter-city relationships at the global level, as these relationships provide the 'glue' of the world economy in their view. The global economy has to be understood, they point out, as a 'space of flows' (Castells, 1996), rather than merely as a constellation of centres of economic power, as was implicit in Friedmann's world-city hypothesis and partly also in the foundational global-city scholarship. In strictly geographical terms, rethinking the relationship between cities and globalization in terms of flows and networks entails relativizing the importance of conventional topographical analysis in favour of a topological view which looks at relations of inter-connectivity amongst urban centres rather than at their position in a rigidly hierarchical space. This shows the importance of this contribution, which has added a trans-state and meta-geographical perspective to world-city research. In Peter Taylor's words:

> the modern world system is defined by its networks, despite being largely studied through its mosaic of states. For any reasonable advance in our theorizing of the world-system, we need to consider systemic networks much more seriously than hitherto. (Taylor, 2000: 29)

Empirical evidence of the network-centred perspective on world cities is provided by Taylor himself, who concentrates his attention on the top ten world cities, looking at the presence/absence of the most important firms specializing in producer services. His findings also confirm the leadership of world cities such as New York and London. The main novelty in this analysis is the different positionality of world cities in their respective geographical regions. New York's hegemony seems to be unchallenged in North America, with Chicago and Los Angeles positioned in a much lower position. In East Asia, owing to its geographical extension and political fragmentation alike (while North America is centred on the USA), Tokyo, Hong Kong and Singapore have similar areas of influence. An intermediate position is held by London, which exerts relative influence over Western Europe, due to its geographical but also political insularity, as well as its substantial detachment from continental Europe (which has become explicit after the recent 'Brexit' vote), allowing Frankfurt and Paris – the economic capitals of the two largest national economies of the Eurozone – to hold a position which is not distant from the elite of world cities (Taylor, 2004).

While the work of Peter Taylor has illuminated the shaping of inter-city networks from the viewpoint of multinational corporations and their locational behaviours, in the early 2000s Michael Peter Smith threw light on another manifestation of the networked world-city phenomenon, challenging the rigid dichotomy between local and global scales which was still prevalent in the 1990s: what he called 'transnational urbanism from below', of which the networks and the connectivities forming across immigrant diasporic communities provided strong evidence (Smith, 2001). This twofold network-centred perspective questioned the conventional understanding of the global-city phenomenon that viewed global cities as territorial entities concentrating economic-political functions and powers. The relational approach, which appeared later, lays emphasis on flows and circulation rather than on networks and connectivities, and represents a further attempt at making sense of urban globalization as a fluid process involving a process of societalization, even though the attention is focused mainly on the elite level. Before engaging with the relational approach, however, it is worth paying attention to an emerging way of looking at the structuring function of global urbanization from a multi-polar perspective.

The global city-regions

Since the early 2000s, the field of urban studies has witnessed a burgeoning body of scholarship investigating the rise of the so-called global city-regions at a time of increasingly multicentric globalization. This phase is marked by the rise of new economic players in the world economy, such as the global powerhouses of the so-called BRICS, plus a number of second-tier emerging economies in Africa, Asia and South America. All these countries boast vast urban agglomerations where there is a concentration of socio-economic resources of great value from the perspective of global competition: from Mumbai to Shanghai, from São Paulo to Lagos, from Mexico City to Jakarta, to name just a few examples of urban giants in the global South located in countries with high economic growth rates. In these countries, the concomitant effect associated with processes of economic globalization, the rationalization of infrastructure and the large inflows of population from the rural regions has allowed megacities to emerge as engines of national economies and attractors of human capital, as well as of public and private investments (Rodríguez-Pose, 2008).

This view of mega-urban regions as engines of growth is in contrast to previous understandings of the phenomenon of urban primacy and gigantism in what at the time was called the 'third world', where rapid demographic growth was generally seen in a negative light as a sign of economic inefficiency and weak infrastructure. In the 1960s, this widespread conviction led many countries – both in the North and the South of the world – to adopt policies of dispersal in order to avoid the supposed disadvantages associated with urban size, a view which at that time economist William Alonso was already criticizing in a somehow prescient way, arguing that 'there is no basis for the belief that primacy or overurbanization *per se* is detrimental to the efficiency goal of economic development. There are good grounds for believing in increasing returns to urban size' (Alonso, 1968: 4). However, recent times have witnessed not just a straightforward return to one-city gigantism, but rather the pursuit of inter-urban aggregation. In China, in the last decade, the national government has committed to developing thirteen multicentric megalopolises, as a result of the functional aggregation of large metro areas and other cities of varying sizes (Economist Intelligence Unit, 2012). One of these megalopolises is the Pearl River Delta: generally known as the 'world factory' due to the unprecedented expansion of manufacturing industry over the last three decades, and the related demographic boom experienced since the 1990s, this urban region has nine cities (Shenzhen, Dongguan, Huizhou, Zhuhai, Zhongshan, Jiangmen, Guangzhou, Foshan and Zhaoqing) whose overall population currently amounts to 42 million people and is expected to rise to 80 million by 2030.

Western European countries have a longer tradition of polycentric urban regions, even though their growth potential is limited by the lack of non-urbanized space and by stagnant demographic rates. This does not mean, however, that national governments and EU institutions are not investing in initiatives aimed at strengthening inter-urban interdependence, such as those following in the wake of the European Spatial Development Perspective initiative launched by the European Commission in 1999. Extant polycentric city-regions in Europe are essentially of two types. One type takes form around a core city playing a role of functional aggregation and symbolic reference for cities of smaller size gravitating around it: for example, the southeast of England, centred on London, the Paris region of Île-de-France, and the urban region of the Italian north-west, centred on Milan and Turin. The second type of mega city-region is more authentically polycentric: the Dutch Randstad, involving the cities of Amsterdam, The

Hague, Utrecht and Rotterdam; the centre-northern part of Belgium gravitating around the urban quadrilateral of Brussels-Leuven-Ghent-Antwerp, where there is the highest concentration of national wealth; the Rhine-Ruhr region, comprising ninety cities of different sizes, none of them holding a dominant position, often regarded as an example of an authentically multicentric megalopolis (Hall and Pain, 2006). The USA has two outstanding examples of mega city-regions: the vast urbanized area surrounding the sprawled urban region of Los Angeles, famously defined as 'post-metropolis' by geographer Edward Soja (Soja, 2000), and the north-eastern urban region (from Washington to Boston), which can be considered an archetype of the city-region, as already in the 1960s French geographer Jean Gottmann had coined the notion of 'megalopolis' with reference to this area (Gottmann, 1962).

Far from being reduced to issues of urban size and demographic power, the city-region theorization is illustrative of the importance acquired by agglomeration economies of both specialization and diversification. The former were famously theorized by Alfred Marshall, subsequently becoming the conceptual base of industrial districts theory – the idea that a local productive system benefits from firms and labour markets specializing in the same type of production, thus favouring relations of mutual trust and collaboration and the exchange of tacit knowledge (Celata and Rossi, 2009). Within the industrial districts literature of the 1980s and the 1990s, neo-Marshallian economies were particularly found in regional spaces characterized by small and medium-sized towns. On the other hand, Jane Jacobs famously theorized the fact that the vitality of urban economies lies in their sectoral diversification which stimulates local competition (Jacobs, 1969). The distinguishing feature of urban post-Fordist economies is the fact that they bring together these two apparently contradictory agglomeration phenomena. As Allen Scott, a leading proponent of the global city-region, puts it:

large cities, as a result, are invariably important centres of resourceful-
ness and invention for all sectors of production, but especially for post-
Fordist industries where the basic conditions leading to these outcomes
are so abundantly concentrated. Finally, supercharged growth is reinforced by the frequent development of multiple industrial clusters or
complexes in any one city-region, particularly where strong spillover
effects flow between the different sectors involved. (Scott, 2001:
819–20)

In conclusion, contemporary global city-regions exemplify the
capacity of cities to dynamically reconcile the cumulative, quantitative factor associated with the concentration of economic activities, specialized functions and population (and the related human
capital) with the qualitative dimension linked to the generation of
what is defined 'cognitive capital' in chapter 1, which is generative
of what Marx and a strand of neo-Marxist scholarship have called
'the general intellect' (see chapter 5). This capacity has been emphasized by the advent of globalization, leading the urban phenomenon
to become both a central space of exploitation and a reinvention of
capitalist culture.

DEEPENING CAPITALIST GLOBALIZATION

The shift from the theorization of the global city, centred on the idea of
the global urban phenomenon as a concentration of economically strategic organizations and functions with an associated cumulative effect,
to a perspective of transnationalism, interpreting the contemporary
world as a constellation of actor-networks, has prepared the ground
for a substantial change in the ways in which the city–globalization
nexus has been understood. These changing perspectives are illustrative of the deepening in capitalist globalization, as the remainder of
this chapter will show.

THE POLICY MOBILITY PARADIGM

The relational perspective builds on the assumption that the process of globalization has set in motion an intensified circulation of ideas, information, knowledge, institutional practices and urban development imaginaries. In this context, cities are key nodes within flows of knowledge, ideas and practices, thanks to the role played by intermediary actors and institutions within them. According to the proponents of the relational perspective, the current round of globalization is giving rise to an increasingly unified urban experience at the planetary level, mainly due to the heightened mobility of urban development and regeneration policies (McCann, 2011). In concrete terms, this means that in recent times cities located in different regional settings across the globe have been transformed by either active or passive reception of policy catchwords and related operational frameworks imported from 'elsewhere'. This process of circulation and reception has been enabled not only by communication and information technologies, but also by the growing hegemony of neoliberalism being mobilized as a 'mobile technology', that is to say as 'a logic of governing that migrates and is selectively taken up in diverse political contexts' (Ong, 2007: 3). The spatial imaginaries associated with allegedly successful 'models' of urban development and regeneration have thus been adopted by economic-political elites across the world, often with the intermediation of national and supranational governmental actors, through qualitatively differentiated modalities, reflecting contingent strategies of economic development. Far from theorizing an urban-political landscape homogenized by the reception of global imaginaries, this perspective emphasizes processes of hybridization, transmutation and variegation arising from the circulation of a global geo-economic institutional logic and its adaptation to different institutional settings, economic-political conditions and cultural-ideological structures (Brenner et al., 2010). In a recent book, Jamie Peck and Nik Theodore have investigated the ways in which policies of participatory budgeting that were originally experimented with in a progressive vein in Porto Alegre in Brazil, becoming for some time a flagship policy of left-leaning municipal governments across the globe, have gradually been assimilated within the neoliberal logic of accountability through the process of circulation (Peck and Theodore, 2015).

The notion of mobility does not imply an idea of horizontal space where flows of knowledge freely intersect each other. On the contrary, according to this view, a narrow set of actors and institutions located in key capitalist countries regulates the traffic of information, ideas and urban development policies. Despite the shaping of a more multipolar world in terms of wealth production, the USA still boasts unrivalled concentrations of powerful institutions generating strategic, exportable knowledge (foundations, private and government research institutes, globally renowned universities, consulting firms), thus retaining their hegemony as exporter of ideas and models of societal well-being and economic development. Public policy being imported from this culturally dominant nation-state mobilizes representations of contemporary cities (global, entrepreneurial, creative, sustainable, resilient, smart) as well as specific aspects of the urban living environments: from housing policy to the design of public space, from social welfare to culture-led regeneration, from business improvement districts to the renewal of slums (or *favelas, villas miserias, bidonvilles,* as they are called in different countries) and deprived neighbourhoods.

The urban experience is, therefore, deeply forged by the strengthening of globalization as a phenomenon of intensified policy circulation. This mobility process takes place in a context of global capitalism characterized by the variegated neoliberalization of urban development. On the one hand, the circulation of urban development models has homogenizing effects at the urban scale, as all cities aspire to become smarter and more creative, sustainable and resilient. On the other hand, place-specific institutional arrangements and the wider national contexts still play a decisive role, thus producing phenomena of hybridization with urban development models that are expressions of globalized structures of thinking and action. Within this dynamic, neoliberalism has proven to be a 'mobile technology' of government particularly suited to accommodating the intricacies of contemporary societies: it exerts a planetary hegemony through coercive modes of rule (for instance, dictating the privatization of public services and the implementation of budget cutbacks), but also through the pursuit of ideals of civic responsibilization and active citizenship (Marinetto, 2003), as well as the cooptation of alternative subjectivities such as sexual minorities and other communities traditionally inclined to transgression and even rebellion (from squatters to artistic communities). This ambivalence of neoliberalism explains its success as the institutional engine of globalization, functioning simultaneously as an imperative of growth and a moral regime emphasizing values of participation, diversity and individuality (see chapter 3).

As already mentioned, the process of travel, recognition and legitimization of neoliberal policies and the related culture of capitalism is perpetuated by a wide range of intermediating actors and institutions: foundations promoting economic development, professional networks and lobbies, and a number of public and private actors concerned with urban issues (Peck, 2010). The process of dissemination at the world scale is conventionally understood as 'policy transfer' within the mainstream political science literature and has been redefined as 'policy mobility' in contemporary critical urban studies, laying emphasis on the process of reinvention associated with the circulation of ideas and policies across the globe. In this sense, scholars interested in the policy mobility phenomenon speak of inter-city 'relationality' as the glue of urban globalization (McCann and Ward, 2010).

The idea of the creative city as theorized by Richard Florida (see chapter 3) is a typical example of policy mobility. Cities across the globe have incorporated the creative-city policy rationale into their urban governance and planning strategies, often merely relabelling pre-existing initiatives of urban regeneration (Ponzini and Rossi, 2010). This process of incorporation and institutional translation is not often acknowledged by the proponents of mainstream theories of creative urbanism. In the second edition of his bestseller book on the creative class, Richard Florida has included a chapter in which he draws attention to the 'global reach' acquired by the creative-class discourse in the last decade (since the publication of the first edition of his book). However, his interpretation avoids clarifying the active role of dissemination played by US-based institutions in spreading the creative-city discourse across the globe (Florida, 2012). In his account, the global circulation of creative-city policies is treated as a natural process, stemming from the spontaneous adoption of these ideas by enlightened local administrations and other public and private actors. In a critical assessment of Florida's ideas in their original formulation, Allen Scott noted the evident contradiction between the normative intonation of the creative-class theory and the lack of attention towards institutional issues of implementation (Scott, 2006). Along related lines, from a policy-mobility perspective, one can observe today how in more recent times Richard Florida has overlooked the phenomenon of hegemonic policy circulation behind the 'global reach' acquired by the creative-city framework in relation to the functioning of globalization as a space of flows.

In sum, the policy mobility perspective represents an advanced attempt at capturing the process of socialization brought on by the circulation and reception of urban development policies and related geographical imaginaries. Its contribution to a deeper understanding of the phenomenon of global urbanization has been decisive. At the same time, this paradigm has strong limitations from the perspective adopted here dealing with cities *in* global capitalism. The process of socialization in the policy-mobility thesis and related strands of research is limited essentially to the elite level, while neoliberalism is viewed as a somewhat external force moving across the globe. This book, on the contrary, aims to show how neoliberalism has to be understood as a constitutive element of global capitalism, whose main imperative – the entrepreneurialization of society and the self – particularly fits with the knowledge-intensive constitution of contemporary urban capitalist economies, as we will see particularly in chapter 5. Moreover, the policy-mobility thesis entails the persistence of a 'centre' in the globalized world, in which the dominant governmental rationality originates and where processes of policy transfer customarily start. While this is still the case in many respects in the dissemination of conventional urban development imaginaries, such as the creative city mentioned earlier, but also in the diffusion of Western forms of cultural colonization such as those analysed in chapter 4, at the same time contemporary communicative and cognitive capitalism is also forged by an increasingly decentralized global discourse in which it is hard to distinguish between a centre and a periphery, an exporting inside and an importing outside. As the concluding parts of chapter 5 will show, the advent of interactive digital technologies has played a central role in globalizing the human experience, in increasingly rhizomatic forms, an aspect overlooked in current policy-mobility research. Finally, from a more contingent perspective, the increasingly weakened legitimacy of the established elites across the globe after the financial crisis of 2008, which will be discussed in the book's concluding chapter, poses significant challenges to the methodological assumptions underlying elite-centred understandings of global urbanization.

THE GLOBAL URBANISM AND PLANETARY URBANIZATION THESES

The first half of the 2010s has seen a revival of debates around cities and globalization, particularly in the wake of path-breaking theses of planetary urbanization and global urbanism. The concept of global urbanism departs from the postcolonial critique of extant urban scholarship, stressing the need to disrupt rigid dichotomies between the North and the South (Sheppard et al., 2013). While attention towards the city–capitalism nexus has been rather limited, as urban political economists have pointed out (Peck, 2015), postcolonial urbanism can have important implications, especially in methodological terms, for the ways in which we think about the economic-political geographies of urbanization in capitalist societies.

On the other hand, the notion of planetary urbanization proposed by Neil Brenner in a series of publications that appeared since 2013, most of them co-authored with Swiss urbanist Christian Schmid, explicitly engages with the reconfiguration of urbanization in relation to global capitalism. In their work, Brenner and Schmid (2014) develop their argument by critically examining the 'urban age' thesis that originated with the United Nations but is now commonplace with both the wider public and academic urbanists, according to which approximately two-thirds of the world's population will be urbanized by 2030. Brenner and Schmid criticize this demography-based thesis as empiricist but also scientifically weak (it relies on heterogeneous datasets provided by nation-states), proposing as an alternative the concept of 'planetary urbanization'. This concept is based on Henri Lefebvre's idea that the traditional urban/rural dichotomy will be overcome by the explosion of urbanization processes based on the dialectical confrontation between concentration, extension and differentiation. In doing so, Brenner and Schmid refuse the primacy of density and agglomeration as distinctive traits of urbanity (Brenner and Schmid, 2014 and 2015). Their attention is particularly focused on 'extended urbanization', which they perceive as the main novelty associated with the deepening of global urbanization processes:

> [W]e propose that the historical and contemporary geographies of urban transformation encompass much broader, if massively uneven, territories and landscapes, including many that may contain relatively small, dispersed or minimal populations, but where major socio-

economic, infrastructural and socio-metabolic metamorphoses have occurred precisely in support of, or as a consequence of, the everyday operations and growth imperatives of often-distant agglomerations. For this reason, the moment of concentrated urbanization is inextricably connected to that of *extended urbanization*. (Brenner and Schmid, 2015: 167; emphasis in the original)

The underlying conceptualization of the relationship between cities and capitalism is centred, on the one hand, on the idea of cities as interconnecting nodes supplying logistical functions and a host of infrastructures that are crucial to the circulation of goods, semi-finished products and raw materials across the world. On the other hand, it also centres on the conceptualization of capital accumulation as a process of dispossession involving the enclosure of land and the privatization of common resources and goods:

extended urbanization is intimately intertwined with the violence of accumulation by dispossession (often automated and enforced by state institutions) through which non-commodified modes of social life are destabilized and articulated to global spatial divisions of labour and systems of exchange. (Ibid.)

While Brenner and Schmid in their tripartite conceptualization of contemporary urbanization processes recognize the persistent importance of concentrated forms of urbanization, as well as of differential urbanization, they emphasize the 'planetary urbanization' thesis and the underlying conceptualization of capitalism as a colonizing process of capitalist exploitation of previously non-capitalist forms of life, enabled by the functioning of the neoliberal regime of societal governance. This conceptualization of capitalism particularly draws on David Harvey's theorization of 'accumulation by dispossession', a notion that he has elaborated within his general conception of neoliberal capitalism as a manifestation of 'new imperialism', appropriating common goods, such as land and natural resources, through the perpetual continuation of primitive accumulation (Harvey, 2003; see chapter 5 for a more detailed analysis of this thesis). While this understanding of capitalism and related forms of urbanization captures the logic of what is occurring in emerging national economies and regions witnessing processes of capitalist expansion (China being the most prominent example), this interpretation relies on an 'inert' conception of the common good and of capitalism itself. Rather, as Hardt and Negri (2009: 133–42) have pointed out, contemporary capitalism still relies primarily on value production, but it does so by exploiting 'biopolitical labour': the vast array of knowledge, affects and social relations that are external to capital but that capital appropriates by subsuming society and life itself within the capitalist process. In this context, in their view, urban environments – particularly those characterized by dense relations of cooperation and thus capable of producing thick externalities – provide capitalist production with an 'artificial common' created by affective labour. This conception of capitalism throws light on the surplus value generated by socially and institutionally thick urban settings, where there is a concentration of institutions, social relations and cooperative forms of life. From this perspective, dominant patterns of knowledge-intensive urbanism, such as those epitomized by the mainstream notions of creative and smart cities, do not appear merely as an 'empty rhetoric' mobilized by neoliberal regimes of urban governance in order to 'sell the city' (Wiig, 2016), or as a disciplinary technique aimed at regulating social behaviour in turbulent urban environments (Vanolo, 2014). Rather, they should be understood as hegemonic projects (Jessop, 1997) mobilized by politico-economic elites who are appropriating the socio-affective externalities of urban environments (Rossi, 2016).

In an article discussing the limits of the planetary urbanization and global urbanism theses, Allen Scott and Michael Storper have correctly stressed the persisting importance of agglomeration for capitalist economies in a context of post-Fordism (Scott and Storper, 2015) and – one might add, drawing on Hardt and Negri (2009) – of bio-political production. In times of post-recession, cities across the world are witnessing an economic renaissance of the urban, particularly due to the role played by high-tech firms in contemporary capitalism, as discussed in chapter 1, but also due to larger processes of economic valorization, such as those customarily known as the 'sharing' economy (Stein, 2015). Despite their social impact in terms of production of new urban inequalities (a rise in housing prices and related gentrification dynamics, deregulation of labour and self-exploitative mechanisms, monopoly power exerted by a handful of digital corporations), both urban high-tech and sharing economies are nourished by intense socio-affective relations, encouraged by the dense urban environments of inner-city areas that are prominent in large cities. The biopolitical dimension of capitalist production and related forms of urbanization is overlooked, not only within accounts of planetary urbanization but also within larger understandings of capitalism centred on ideas of dispossession, enclosure and colonization, as discussed earlier in this chapter. However, the comparative method advocated by post-colonial urbanists, but dismissed by Scott and Storper's accusation of lack of conceptual abstraction and of particularism, should be more carefully re-evaluated. The comparative urbanism embraced under the aegis of the postcolonial critique is intended to uncover the particularities of places and the irreducible diversity of urban development pathways, especially from the viewpoint of the global North–South divide (Robinson, 2011). In this vein, comparative urbanism rejects the idea of normative knowledge, contrary to conventional comparative scholarship within the nomothetic social sciences, which tend to construct typologies, models and hierarchical classifications. From the perspective adopted here, postcolonial emphasis on the diversity of forms of life and on the need to decentralize our understanding of the urban condition provides useful conceptual tools to analyse what is understood here as the global capitalist city in the biopolitical age. For this reason, it is useful to consider provocative solutions to the West-centrism of the social sciences being put forward by postcolonial authors, such as 'new geographies of theory' (Roy, 2009) and 'Southern theory' (Connell, 2007; Comaroff and Comaroff, 2012). Moreover, in a recently published article, Jennifer Robinson has refined the post-colonial formulation of comparative urban studies, drawing on both the Marxist notion of 'real abstraction' and the Deleuzian idea of 'difference and repetition' (Robinson, 2016). This refined conceptualization of comparative urbanism avoids the risk of particularism that was under-mining her 'ordinary city' thesis (Robinson, 2006), offering a more robust methodological account centred on the idea of urban contexts as interconnected and interrelated 'singularities' subject to 'repeated instances' of development and capitalist modernization, which enables us to understand in innovative ways persisting processes of Western homogenization such as those analysed in chapter 4 of this book.

In urban studies, however, the interest in comparative methodolo-gies has not been limited to the postcolonial strand of critique and thinking. The interest in comparative methodologies has stemmed also from reflections over the embrace of relational understandings of urban development trajectories, which are alternative or complementary to territorial views of urbanism (Ward, 2010), as discussed earlier in this chapter. This leads us to underline another aspect overlooked in Scott and Storper's critique of comparative urbanism: the role played by policy discourse in the production of contemporary global urbanism. Refusing understandings of city politics as a bounded and self-sufficient realm, the relational perspective postulates the increasing interconnect-edness of cities across the globe, particularly as a consequence of the cross-national circulation of public discourse and urban development models. This position is indebted to cultural political economy, as has been theorized and empirically applied to the study of hegemonic projects and accumulation strategies at different levels (particularly the urban) by Bob Jessop (2004) and other UK-based scholars. The literature exploring the policy mobility phenomenon in contemporary cities across the world has shown how the circulation of policy imperatives entails a process of transmutation into different economic-political contexts, rather than of rigidly bilateral export, transfer and adoption. This phenomenon decisively contributes to making the urban experience unified on a global scale, producing an increasingly transnational urban governmentality (cf. Ferguson and Gupta, 2002). However, as pointed out in the previous section, attention to policy discourse is not sufficient, as its limitation is to confine our perspective to the role and conduct of elites, failing to take into account the increasingly rhizomatic characterization of global capitalism at a time of ubiquitous interaction technologies enabling the entrepreneurialization of both society as a whole and the self, as chapter 5 of this book will analyse in greater detail.

CONCLUSION

It is now widely accepted that cities and globalization are inextricable phenomena of our time. Over the last quarter of a century, a growing number of urban scholars have dedicated their energies to the investigation of the relationship between cities and globalization: from the pioneers of world-city research (John Friedmann, Saskia Sassen, Michael Peter Smith and Peter Taylor being the most influential authors) to the proponents of the more recent planetary urbanization and global urbanism theses, such as Neil Brenner and the postcolonial scholars. Less attention has been devoted to an accurate reflection on the ways in which these different interpretations of the city–globalization relationship shed light on different conceptualizations of capitalism. This book and this chapter more specifically are intended to shed light on the varied understandings of capitalism, on the one hand, through the lens of the relationship between cities, urbanization processes and the socio-cultural phenomenon of urbanism, and, on the other hand, through the lens of globalization.

Early views on world cities as strongholds of the global economy, thanks to their attraction as the headquarters of multinational corporations, international organizations and the most advanced business services, expressed a view of capitalism as a highly polarized phenomenon in both socio-spatial and economic terms. At this time, capitalist globalization was interpreted as a process centred on the hegemonic role of economically powerful actors. The supply of producer services in which global cities specialized was associated with this presence of powerful actors. Chapter 4 will begin by looking at how especially early conceptualizations of globalization and the globalizing urban phenomenon were conceived in relation to colonizing forces at the cultural level. In this context, global cities were represented as magnets of capitalist power and its cultural representation. This idea of uniformization is still a defining feature of the globalization process, but over time it has been complemented with other descriptions, where global urbanization is regarded as a socially diffused, internally differentiated and constantly evolving phenomenon nurtured by movement, circulation and flows of people, knowledge and discourse. Despite the relevance of both the policy-mobility paradigm and the planetary urbanization thesis, the remainder of this book aims to move beyond their conceptualizations of global urbanization, for the reasons illustrated earlier in this chapter. The following chapter will show how global capitalism has been shaped by a process of continuous interchange between cities and neoliberalism, the latter being understood as an entity that has grown into the living tissue of the capitalist city. Today's urban centrality in global capitalism derives from this intimate link between cities and neoliberalism, preceding the advent of globalization itself, at least in the way we are accustomed to knowing it. Moreover, the diffusion of colonizing forces across the globe, discussed in chapter 4, shows the continued dominance of Western culture, but also the need to embrace a place-sensitive understanding of global processes. Following that, chapter 5 enters into the discussion of contemporary biopolitical society in its urban form. It does so by offering an ambivalent picture of capitalist urbanism, one in which the negative subjection of society (through the normalization of the regime of austerity at the city-wide level) coexists with its affirmative mobilization through economic experiments that exploit the communicative and cognitive potential of contemporary cities, thus reasserting capitalism's promise of happiness and prosperity. Thanks to its ductility and its own ambivalence, the neoliberal governmental rationality – with its emphasis on the entrepreneurialization of society and the self – acts as a unifying, aggregating force within this stratification of economic processes, forms of life, hegemonies and historical temporalities that characterizes global capitalism in the biopolitical age.

3 | Continuities ————————————

NEOLIBERALISM AS A LIVING ENTITY

Neoliberalism is commonly understood as a political and social philosophy that originally emerged as a heterodox line of economic thinking in the 1930s and after the Second World War, becoming hegemonic as an 'art of government' since the economic crisis of the mid-1970s and the consequent dismantling of the Fordist-Keynesian regime of capital accumulation. In the following decade, the fall of the Soviet Union opened the way for the perceived triumph of neoliberal capitalism in the absence of viable alternatives. Neoliberal ideas, therefore, gained ground at a time of economic and geopolitical turmoil between the 1970s and the 1980s. The following two decades saw the expansion of the neoliberal project in both qualitative and quantitative terms: on the one hand, the neoliberal project has deeply restructured existing economic and institutional relations in capitalist societies; on the other hand, it has achieved an increasingly global reach under conditions of advanced globalization, as the previous chapter has shown.

It is now widely acknowledged that cities have played a central role in the ascendancy, consolidation and geographical extension of neoliberalism. This chapter, however, will go beyond a characterization of neoliberalism as a mere set of ideas being adopted at the political level and imported into the public-policy sphere; rather, it shows how the rise of neoliberalism is inscribed within the dynamics of contemporary capitalism and how cities have been crucial to the realization of the neoliberal project, not only as sites of policy implementation but also in a generative sense. Cities are indeed fertile grounds for the entrepreneurialization of society and the self and the 'economization' of life, which characterize advanced liberal societies. The notion of 'urban entrepreneurialism' – its socio-cultural roots and its evolutionary path – has been illustrated in chapter 1 of this book: in brief, it refers to urban governments' capacity to leverage societal resources and stimulate the formation of pro-growth development coalitions, attracting public and private investments to boost local economic growth and create a pro-business environment (Harvey, 1989b). As the previous chapter has illustrated, since the Middle Ages cities have been at the forefront in the entrepreneurialization of society at different levels. The closely interrelated notion of 'economization' refers to the reduction of the citizen and the idea of citizenship itself to the logic of the *Homo oeconomicus*, which conceals the very existence of a public sphere as an autonomous entity from growth-driven economic life (Brown, 2015).

Against that backdrop, this chapter will show how today's close interlinkage between city and neoliberalism is based on a relationship of cross-fertilization. This means that, on the one hand, neoliberalism has drawn on the urban phenomenon and particularly on the way in which this has taken shape within capitalist societies; on the other hand, the urban phenomenon has drawn on the culture of neoliberalism and particularly on its tendency to commodify and spectacularize any aspect of social life. The first section of this chapter briefly introduces the reader to the main conceptual approaches to the study of neoliberalism and of urban neoliberalism more specifically; the second section presents the way in which neoliberalism has incorporated long-term features of the urban phenomenon in capitalist societies. Finally, the third section of the chapter looks at the way in which the urban phenomenon has been reshaped by the advent of neoliberalism itself.

THE CITY-NEOLIBERALISM NEXUS

Why have neoliberal development regimes become so successful in contemporary cities across the world? Two main strands of critical thinking provide us with a response to this question. First, Marxist-inspired urban political economy scholars, particularly those who draw inspiration from Henri Lefebvre and David Harvey and their theorization of the role of the built environment in the secondary circuit of capital (see chapter 1), associate the ascent of urban neoliberalism with the entrepreneurialization of governance structures in a context characterized by the increasing profitability of urban environments after the decline of Fordism and the consequent process of deindustrialization in the 1970s and the 1980s. From this perspective, neoliberalism has been understood as a hegemonic mode of societal governance and capital accumulation strategy, resorting to supply-side economic policies with the aim of improving the competitiveness of firms and territories, including cities and their economic actors (Brenner and Theodore, 2002).

The second main strand of thinking is formed by scholars inspired by the work of Michel Foucault and particularly by his diagnosis of neoliberal governmentality (Dean, 2010). These scholars look at cities as crucial spaces where one can observe and critically analyse the materialization of neoliberalism as both a political rationality and an art of government being conducted in the name of 'freedom', 'participation' and 'accountability' (Swyngedouw, 2005; Blakeley, 2010). In this context, the adoption of a neoliberal governmental rationality entails the willingness to turn city dwellers into responsible, disciplined and active individuals through the functioning of increasingly more sophisticated and rationalized systems of evaluation, surveillance and education. The more recent work of Giorgio Agamben has built on Foucault's notion of biopolitics to investigate the changing forms of power and sovereignty within totalitarian forms of democracy. Agamben is an

Italian thinker who previously specialized in the study of aesthetics, as well as of twentieth-century German philosophers like Heidegger, Arendt and Benjamin, who had experienced the Nazi regime in very different ways (Heidegger was actively involved as a university rector, while Arendt and Benjamin were both forced into exile). Agamben's influence on urban scholarship has been more limited compared with other fields in the social sciences (such as geopolitics, international relations and migration studies). However, the contemporary reception of the notion of neoliberalism is heavily indebted to his theory of the *Homo sacer* (Agamben, 1998). For instance, the influential work of anthropologist Aihwa Ong has picked up on Agamben's notion of exception as a fundamental principle of sovereign rule, in order to analyse the neoliberal politics of both including and excluding exception within the emerging economies of East Asia (Ong, 2006). Her work, and particularly her notion of neoliberalism as a mobile government technology, has inspired the formulation of key concepts within urban studies, such as those of 'variegated neoliberalization' and 'policy mobility' (see chapters 2 and 5).

The notion of neoliberalism has thus been mobilized within critical urban studies to refer mainly to two distinct but interrelated projects: first, a politico-economic mode of regulation centred on the corporatization of the public sector and the hegemonic imperative of economic growth, embracing an expansionary fiscal policy which incentivizes economic activity through tax cuts on dividends and long-term capital gains; second, a discursive-moral governmental rationality committed to refashioning existing social relationships along competitive, individualistic and communitarian lines. Within critical urban studies and the wider critical social sciences, a growing number of scholars have attempted to reconcile these lines of thinking by embracing a so-called poststructuralist or cultural political economy approach, which combines the analysis of discursive apparatuses of subject formation with that of economic-political initiatives and related accumulation strategies (Larner, 2000; Jessop, 2002a; Barnett, 2005). More recently, a larger refusal of economistic understandings of neoliberalism and globalization has emerged within urban studies, particularly in the wake of the eruption of postcolonial strands of critique within this field, which have called into question the partiality of West-centric economic reason, drawing attention to the diversity of everyday life in today's 'world of cities' (Robinson, 2006). This has induced urban political economists to interrogate themselves about the generalization of conceptual frameworks that were originally formulated with reference to cities in advanced capitalist and liberal societies (Peck, 2015).

Despite postcolonial criticism and the larger scepticism about the risk of concept-stretching in such a multivalent usage of the notion of neoliberalism, even after the economic collapse of 2008 and the related legitimacy crisis neoliberalism has firmly retained its power as today's hegemonic governmental rationality. At the same time, it continues to be a guiding concept mobilized by critical social scientists – and with particular fervour by urban scholars – dealing with the study of an increasing number of issues, given the social pervasiveness of the neoliberal project.

URBANIZING NEOLIBERALISM

The two-sided relationship of cities with neoliberalism can be observed, in the first instance, by looking at those distinguishing features of the urban experience within advanced economies which have become key aspects of the neoliberal regime of societal governance. In general terms, when public policy was focused on aggregate demand and social welfare, during the Keynesian 'golden age of capitalism', cities were already committed to the imperative of growth. As underlined by specialists of post-war urban politics in the USA (Peterson, 1981; Berg, 2007; Judd and Swanstrom, 2014), this especially applied to US cities, acting in response to federal programmes. Subsequently, the growth imperative has been incorporated into a more coherent political, conceptual and ideological framework, under the banner of the entrepreneurialization of urban governance, which we now recognize as a distinctive trait of 'urban neoliberalism'. More specifically, two aspects historically associated with capitalist cities have played a crucial role within contemporary neoliberal societies: consumption and housing.

THE CONSUMPTION MACHINE

Since the rise of capitalism, urban societies have been characterized by the steady increase of individual consumption. As unrivalled concentrations of vendors and purchasers, cities and larger metropolitan areas have become crucial to the growth of consumption. With the advent of mass production in the twentieth century, now conventionally termed 'Fordism', increasingly standardized forms of consumption gained ground in Western societies and particularly in their cities and metropolitan regions. The twentieth century saw department stores proliferating at the expense of small shops and traditional open-air markets (Sennett, 1976), with early examples in populous and culturally dominant industrial cities such as Paris, New York and Chicago. The society of mass consumerism largely characterized the central stages of the so-called 'golden age of capitalism' during the three decades following the end of the Second World War.

After the economic and geopolitical turbulences of the 1970s, the decline of Fordism and of the related system of mass production paved the way for the advent of a neo-capitalist development pattern – commonly known as post-Fordism – based on lean production on the one hand (particularly represented by Toyota's just-in-time techniques) and on aestheticized consumption, on the other hand. While in the Fordist era, and the so-called golden age of urban-industrial capitalism, mass consumerism was oriented towards the acquisition of durable goods such as the family car, home appliances and furnishings, the post-Fordist era has witnessed the rise of increasingly individualized forms of consumption. Since the early 1980s, capitalist firms have adapted to this new consumption regime by engaging in so-called 'flexible production' (Piore and Sabel, 1984). A 'new spirit of capitalism', founded on the 'commodification of difference' and the 'neutralization of critique', has thus gained ground since the 1970s, in response to the perceived lack of authenticity associated with mass production (Boltanski and Chiapello, 2005).

The qualitative change in the spirit of capitalism has been accompanied by the demographic growth of cities, enabled by the extension of globalization and the advent of 'planetary urbanization' discussed in chapter 2. The expanding process of global urbanization has entailed the formation of a new class of consumers in an increasing number of emerging markets across the world. In the rapidly growing economies of India and China, for instance, the formation of the consumer class has become a priority for public policy. In 2013, the government of China announced a comprehensive urbanization plan, designed to move about 250 million people (approximately equivalent to 80 per cent of the entire US population) currently living in rural environments to rapidly enlarging megacities. These newly built urban districts are intended to trigger a process of economic growth, spurred by the formation of a class of urbanites consuming domestic products and demanding public services. This process of displacement – or China's Great Uprooting, as it has been defined (Johnson, 2013) – is rapidly spreading the new spirit of capitalism beyond the West. As the global consultant agency McKinsey puts it, China currently witnesses the rise of a new class of 'prosperous, more individualistic, and more sophisticated' consumers who are no longer limited to the coastal cities, as this class is increasingly extending its reach over inland cities: 'these consumers seek emotional satisfaction through better taste or higher status, are loyal to the brands they trust, and prefer niche over mass brands' (Barton et al., 2013). The formation of a domestic market of consumers involves a significant rise in wages in China and, as a consequence, the relocation of many multinational companies seeking a cheaper labour force in other Asian countries. In India, the government led by Hindu nationalist Narendra Modi actively encourages this process through the 'Make in India' campaign, based on the reduction of bureaucracy and the improvement of infrastructure. Multinational companies are highly interested in the process, as they 'are enthralled by the potential of the Indian consumer' (Bradsher, 2015), envisioning an economic development trajectory similar to that of China.

Albeit China's and India's urbanization and industrialization programmes may evoke a Keynesian demand-driven approach to economic development in strictly macroeconomic terms, the adoption of a neoliberal rationality of societal governance instils a culture of individualized consumerism into the citizenry of these emerging capitalist economies. In China, recent urbanization plans build on previous processes of societal differentiation and the associated production of new urban inequalities arising from the market-oriented policies adopted since the late 1980s. Economic reform in China implied a weakening of the redistributive policies that had been behind the shaping of mass patterns of consumption in the previous two decades and, in doing so, it widened disparities in purchasing power, thus preparing the ground for the 'revolution in urban consumption' (Davis, 2000) that is currently under way (see also chapter 4).

Neoliberalism has given a threefold contribution to the intensification of individualized and diversified consumerism subjected to the multi-localization strategies of capitalist enterprises. First, neoliberalization policies have allowed globalization to function as a hegemonic force within the world economy, opening markets to foreign direct investment and the import of external commodities from abroad, even in previously state-planned economies such as China and India.

Second, neoliberal policies have triggered processes of commodification involving an increasing number of societal domains, which had been under public control at the time of welfare capitalism, such as health care, transportation, education and professional training (Comaroff and Comaroff, 2000). Under the neoliberal regime, commodification and the related phenomenon of intensive consumerism have affected, therefore, not only conventional consumption goods but also public services and, increasingly, any aspect of everyday life. This commodification of everyday life had been prophesied by Marxist theorist György Lukács in the 1920s, in his theory of reification, by which the commodity is bound to become the 'universal category of society as a whole' (Lukács, 1999: 86). The pervasive commodification entails that we are now customers not only of conventional retail activities such as shops, hotels and department stores, but also of hospitals and schools, as well as of online services, all of which has radically transformed everyday life. Third, as a consequence of the two previous factors, neoliberal governmentality has infused into individuals a culture of competition and social distinction, centred on the pursuit of an 'enterprise society', which is presupposed on the principle of the freedom of the enterprise and the entrepreneur to which the consumer (and the worker) is made subordinate (Lazzarato, 2009).

In a context already characterized by the entrepreneurialization and commodification of everything, capitalist societies have seen the expansion of the technology-based 'sharing economy' in the most disparate fields of social life, such as food, hospitality, mobility, education and money, gradually replacing the traditional service economy. This process has coincided with the shrinkage of the economy brought on by the global recession in Western societies. Under conditions of scarcity, real or perceived, trade liberalization in the service economy and the primacy acquired by the experiential dimension have been key factors in the ascent of the sharing economy (Stein, 2015). In this sector, conventional distinctions between suppliers and consumers of services are blurring, as anyone can be at one and the same time in both roles. The term 'sharing economy' is illusory as things are exchanged on the basis of private ownership rather than shared or co-created on a basis of equality and commonality, as the notion of sharing would entail. In this sense, this phenomenon is revelatory of Adorno's concept of 'exchange society': a society whose aim becomes the production of exchange values per se, as a consequence of interlocked economic, political, psychological and cultural determinants (Adorno, 2004).

While the sharing economy is flourishing also in smaller cities and towns, large cities and metropolitan areas are certainly key sites of this 'exchange society'. Moreover, cities and metropolitan areas are the places witnessing the harshest conflicts linked to this phenomenon. These conflicts have particularly intensified in recent times, reflecting the rapid expansion of the sharing economy. Protests led by cab drivers against the taxi service offered by Uber – a key global player in the sharing economy – have erupted in cities across the world, including Paris, London and Mumbai. Recently, in tourist-dominated cities in Europe, such as Barcelona and Berlin, local governments have introduced tighter regulations on the rental market for temporary homes, in order to limit the distorting effects that the tourism economy has on rent prices and the housing market in general. Compared with the major cities, smaller cities are in many respects in a better position to deal with this phenomenon. In the USA, while New York City opts for restrictive regulations towards online services such as Airbnb, the neighbouring municipality of Jersey City – the second-largest urban centre in the State of New Jersey – plans to adopt legislation legalizing short-term rentals, allowing residents to freely rent their properties even when they are not living in them, but requiring them to pay the same hospitality tax levied on guests at the city's conventional hotels (Chaban, 2015).

The historical functioning of capitalist cities as 'consumption machines' has particularly intensified in a context of cognitive-communicative capitalism. In this form of capitalism, the consumption and circulation of commodities are fully absorbed not only within the firm's value chain, which treats marketing and sales as primary activities and key sources of competitive advantage (Porter, 1985), but within the value chain of society as a whole and of the metropolis most particularly as a central site of biopolitical reproduction (Hardt and Negri, 2009). Contemporary capitalism, therefore, and particularly its post-crisis manifestation, deeply reshaped by previous financial turbulence, has offered the material base for the rise of the sharing economy and the associated pattern of technology-based consumption. Technological consumption is particularly suited for a '24/7 capitalism' (Crary, 2013) in which everyone is required to be relentlessly active and productive, always and everywhere, in constant connection with the outside world through 'smart' technological devices. This condition gives rise to what Maurizio Lazzarato defines 'machinic enslavement': a humans-machines apparatus in which humans and machines are interchangeable parts of a production-communications-consumption circuit that largely exceeds them (Lazzarato, 2014).

In this context, neoliberalism has served as the political-moral engine for the adoption and dissemination of a totalizing life regime in cities across the world. While the experience of consumption in its different stages is immanent in the urban phenomenon and the evolution of capitalism, neoliberalism has embraced the consumption imperative, making it subordinate to the process of commodification and entrepreneurialization of everything in at least three ways. First, the enactment of neoliberal policies has led to the liberalization of trade sectors and services that were previously controlled by professional organizations and are now replaced by the 'entrepreneur of the self': from hospitality to private mobility, from commerce to social care, the recent advent of the sharing economy and related forms of the so-called 'experience economy' draws on pre-existing processes of deregulation and 'entrepreneurialization of the self' in neoliberal societies (see chapter 5).

Second, neoliberalism has revitalized the capitalist culture of private property, extending it to all domains of social life, starting with the housing sector, due to its socio-affective and political value, as will be discussed in this chapter. Third, neoliberalism has championed the idea of the investor citizen (see chapter 1) who is not simply putting away savings over her lifetime, but who commits to extracting a rent out of her possessions. Dominant discursive formations in late neoliberal societies propel the idea that, in response to the shrinkage of social welfare and the volatility of the labour market, it is worth getting a loan from a bank to buy a house or a car whose exchange value can be monetized and possibly reinvested in financial markets. This mechanism reflects the renewed centrality of rent in cognitive capitalism, which makes the distinction between profit and rent increasingly imperceptible (Vercellone, 2008). Indebtedness and financial risk thus entail the subordination of individuals (the worker and the consumer) to a capitalist logic of profit and rent even when they are involved in apparently horizontal mechanisms of collaborative economy.

THE DREAM (AND NIGHTMARE) OF A HOMEOWNERSHIP SOCIETY

Housing in capitalist cities is another societal realm in which commodification precedes neoliberalism but has intensified after its advent, giving rise to a process of mutual reinforcement. Neoliberalism has therefore emphasized a long-term feature of capitalist societies. Historically, the housing sector has acted as a contra-cyclical regulator of economic growth, as testified by the fact that Western economies, such as the US economy above all, have become dependent on high and constantly increasing house prices, particularly in central locations for business and political reasons. However, the vitality of housing markets strictly depends on that of capitalist economies, particularly at the city level, and the specific configuration of urban economies

(Smet, 2016). For instance, it is widely acknowledged today that the tech boom experienced by an elite of US cities after the recession of 2007–9 is reflected in inflationary housing prices, while cities that are not experiencing this boom have persistently stagnant housing markets.

In a context of capitalist urbanization, the segmentation of the housing market reflects both pre-existing and new social divisions (Aalbers and Cristophers, 2014), but also constantly evolving inter-regional inequalities (Longman, 2015). After the Second World War, during the so-called 'golden age of capitalism', the politics of social welfare mitigated the commodification of housing by providing public and subsidized housing. Often located in the working-class areas of industrial cities and towns, this housing is run by state and local authorities (for instance, labelled 'council housing' in the British context). The 1960s and the 1970s saw the peak of state intervention in the housing sector, particularly in Western European countries where social democratic parties had taken the lead in national governments. Britain and Sweden were notable examples in this regard as both countries witnessed ambitious one-million homes programmes, adopted between the mid-1960s and the mid-1970s. However, the crisis of the Keynesian state and the fiscal revolts of the middle and upper classes in the USA led to a quick retreat by the state from direct intervention, paving the way for a renewed belief in private property and self-regulating markets. In the housing sector, two events symbolized the upcoming era of property-based individualism: first, the adoption of Proposition 13 in California in 1978 (when Ronald Reagan was governor), an amendment to the state Constitution ruling that taxation could not exceed 1 per cent of the property value; second, in the United Kingdom the launch of the 'Right to Buy' initiative in 1980, allowing tenants living in state-owned housing to purchase their dwellings, a flagship policy of the new Conservative era led by Prime Minister Margaret Thatcher (Jones and Murie, 2006).

The importance of Proposition 13 in California and the Right to Buy policy in Britain lies in the fact that these initiatives symbolized a larger reversal in macroeconomic policy in capitalist countries during the 1980s. The so-called Reaganomics in the USA and the neoliberal policy course embraced by Margaret Thatcher shared an emphasis on 'supply-side' policies, aiming to incentivize businesses and the workforce as a way of bolstering the economy. This was in direct contrast to the demand management of the Keynesian era, based on the strategic use of the multiplier effect of government spending. A pillar of the new supply-side strategy was the alleviation of fiscal pressure on businesses and capital holders: a measure that was accompanied by shrinkage of the welfare state, deregulation of the labour market and privatization of government-owned enterprises in key sectors such as transportation, energy and communication. In the United Kingdom, Margaret Thatcher adopted such policies, with a special emphasis on the reduction of labour union power. These policy ideas and recipes were widely embraced across the world, from advanced capitalist countries (France and Japan were amongst the first to join Britain in the process of privatization in the 1980s) to countries in the global South, which were urged to adopt 'structural adjustment programmes' by Washington-based lending authorities such as the International Monetary Fund and the World Bank.

In the neoliberal context, the alleviation of the tax base, which undermined the proportional and progressive principle of taxation adopted in advanced capitalist countries during the post-war decades, has never vanished. Economist Paul Krugman has recently noted how all candidates for the presidential nomination in the Republican Party propose tax cuts for the wealthy, promising to give a stimulus to the wider economy (Krugman, 2015). However, it is not only conservative politicians that embrace what Krugman and other left-leaning critics of supply-side economic policies define as 'voodoo economics' (see Harvey, 1989c). As the idea that public opinion favoured tax cuts over public spending became the new orthodoxy, fiscal relaxation policies that had been introduced by conservative governments were never questioned by centre-left politicians proposing the so-called 'Third Way' in the 1990s, such as Tony Blair in the UK (see Giddens, 1998), Bill Clinton in the USA and Gerard Schröder in Germany. As a result, demand-driven policies inspired by Keynesian economics have been systematically marginalized and excluded from the viable alternatives, at least until the financial crash of 2008. The financial crisis and the related 'global recession' (or the 'Great Contraction', as it is also known) have shaken widespread convictions in the public-policy sphere, particularly the unconditional belief in economic deregulation. In the aftermath of the economic crisis, Keynesian approaches came to the fore within public debates over the post-recession transition. In 2009, President Obama announced a new deal based on the stimulation of the green economy through an increase in government spending, while the Federal Reserve managed to stop the negative spiral of the financial crisis through a budget deficit policy supporting demand in a context characterized by private disinvestment in key sectors like housing itself.

At the same time, however, on the other side of the Atlantic, another idea has gained wide currency, becoming dominant amongst policymakers in the European Union: the so-called 'expansionary austerity', an apparent oxymoron that postulates positive effects in terms of economic growth brought on by systematic budget cutbacks (Blyth, 2012). The management of the Eurozone crisis has been conducted by adopting the expansionary austerity rationale, thus re-establishing neoliberal governmentality on apparently novel bases, but in continuity with the austerity policies of the late 1970s and the early 1980s. As in its early stages, this neoliberalist approach relies on budget cutbacks and the shrinkage of the social welfare system. A peculiar mix of German ordo-liberalism, recommending policies of fiscal retrenchment, and American neoliberalism, dictating governmental downsizing, has shaped the EU context in the aftermath of the global economic crisis (but see chapter 5 for a critique of the nation-centred understanding of neoliberalism).

However, once the austerity drive became less of an imperative in light of a seeming end to the recession, government leaders again started promising tax reductions and other measures aimed at increasing the number of owner-occupiers in the housing market. This expansionary fiscal policy is pursued through typically supply-side policies like tax cuts, rather than through an increase of public spending to stimulate the aggregate demand as in the Keynesian model. This is illustrated by Britain and Italy, two large economies and populous countries in the European Union, both characterized by high homeownership rates, a phenomenon that has been momentarily affected by the freezing of housing markets caused by the financial crisis, especially in Britain, whose percentage rate was well above 70 per cent prior to the crisis and dropped to 64 per cent in 2013, according to Eurostat data (Italy's homeownership rate has remained more constantly above 70 per cent). In order to tackle this situation, Britain's right-wing government has announced its intention to reduce housing benefit entitlements for young individuals demanding access to privately rented housing and, at the same time, to resume Margaret Thatcher's Right to Buy policy, thus reviving her idea of a 'home-owning democracy'.

In Italy, the centre-left government led by Matteo Renzi – a young, ambitious politician explicitly drawing inspiration from Tony Blair's Third Way – has put forward a plan to abolish the municipal tax on property used as primary residence, starting from 2016. Critics of this policy proposal have pointed out that wealthy households would especially benefit from this tax cut. However, the political cartel supporting this abolition has been firmly bipartisan, as the measure is obviously popular with the electorate. The suppression of this tax had indeed been decided by the centre-left government led by Romano Prodi in 2006–8, then enacted by Silvio Berlusconi when he was the head of the right-wing government in 2008–10. The tax was eventually reintroduced by the technocratic government led by the former EU commissioner Mario Monti in 2011, when the European Central Bank urged the Italian government to adopt stringent measures of fiscal rigour. In Britain, one can detect a similarly instrumental use of homeownership. In an electoral speech given in April 2015, David Cameron declared 'The dream of a property-owning democracy is alive and well', while a few months later in a newspaper article co-authored with George Osborne – the Chancellor of the Exchequer in his government – he wrote: 'we will transform Britain: from a lower-home ownership, higher-tax, higher-housing-benefit country to one that encourages home ownership, reduces taxes, lowers housing benefit and builds more homes' (Cameron and Osborne, 2015).

A distinguishing trait of neoliberalism's bipartisan consensus among the mainstream parties, therefore, has been the pursuit of higher homeownership rates as a proof of economic well-being and societal stability. The bipartisan consensus over the goal of an expanded homeownership deserves particular attention. Albeit conventionally associated with conservative culture, particularly in Britain, having been popularized by former Prime Minister Anthony Eden in 1946 and then revitalized and translated into a housing strategy by Margaret Thatcher, the idea of a 'property-owned democracy' has a much more ambivalent history (Ronald, 2008). Over time, this has been embraced not only by advocates of free-market ideologies and social conservatism, but also by different kinds of social liberals: from Fabian socialists in the early twentieth century to philosopher John Rawls and his followers in more recent times, who saw it as a model for the advancement of egalitarian distributive objectives, avoiding the authoritarian character of the interventionist state. On the other hand, even ultra-neoliberal organizations such as the Ludwig von Mises Institute – a US-based think tank committed to disseminating the ideas of the Austrian School of neoclassical economics and the related social philosophy of market libertarianism and the minimal state – disregard homeownership ideologies as a manifestation of a pervasive power exerted by governments over the free choice of individuals and market forces (French, 2010). This position is not surprising as, from a strictly capitalist viewpoint, it is questionable whether homeownership positively contributes to economic growth, as the fact of being homeowner inhibits the residential mobility of the workforce, in contrast to the functioning of increasingly mobile societies and the idea that 'jobs follow places' within technology-based, creative economies (Florida, 2012).

In the neoliberal age, however, despite the evident contradictions, the idea of a homeownership society has remained a largely uncontested orthodoxy within the mainstream political parties and public opinion in Western countries until the bursting of the housing bubble in 2007 and the financial collapse of 2008. Conservative leaders were in the forefront in associating their leadership mandate with the pursuit of a 'nation of home owners' (Saunders, 1990), particularly in electoral times: from Bush's idea of an 'ownership society' to French President Sarkozy's willingness to turn France into 'un pays de propriétaires'. While the goal of a homeownership society has become a distinguishing trait of the conservative field, centre-left leaders have also adopted this goal with enthusiasm, as illustrated by the Clinton administration in the mid-1990s, within the framework of the 'National Homeownership Strategy'. President Clinton authored an introduction to this policy document, celebrating the virtues of homeownership:

> for millions of America's working families throughout our history, owning a home has come to symbolize the realization of the American Dream [...] Expanding homeownership will strengthen our nation's families and communities, strengthen our economy, and expand this country's great middle class. Rethinking the dream of homeownership for America's working families can prepare our nation to embrace the rich possibilities of the twenty-first century. (Clinton, 1995)

The policy document mentioned the adoption of 'financing strategies, fuelled by the creativity and resources of the private and public sectors' driven 'by a commitment to increase opportunities for homeownership for more families, particularly for low- and moderate-income and minority families' (US Department of Housing and Urban Development, 1995: 39). The proposed strategies ('cut transactions costs', 'reduce downpayment and mortgage costs', 'increase availability of financing') proved to be illusory in a context characterized by the adoption of subprime mortgages and other secondary loan schemes offered to low-income homebuyers under conditions that many commentators framed in terms of 'predatory lending' affecting the poor (Squires, 2004). In this context, US city governments enthusiastically adhered to the renewed belief in the benefits of homeownership that characterized the neoliberal era, with the increase of homeownership rates being seen as a sign of economic health and competitiveness by city mayors and mainstream policymakers (Basolo, 2007).

Another centre-left political leader who enthusiastically embraced the ideal of homeownership was Tony Blair, the proponent of the 'Third Way' when he was prime minister of the United Kingdom from 1997 to 2007. According to *The Financial Times*, Blair's interest in stressing the value of homeownership stemmed from his 'desire not be outflanked over housing by the Tories' (Blitz, 2005). Blair's attitude clearly showed the cultural hegemony that conservatives have gained in Britain and elsewhere over the idea of society to be pursued by public policy. However, the same *FT* article also reported that in his embrace of the ideal of homeownership Blair had to cope with other key members of the Labour government who prioritized policies supporting publicly funded, large-scale house-building programmes. Political contrasts within his own party – along with the fear of proposing a pale copy of the conservative policies – did not prevent Blair from publicly celebrating the virtues of a homeownership society:

We believe we can get home ownership up to 80 percent. Certainly hundreds of thousands more people should be able to own their homes. (Blair, 2005, quoted in Blitz, 2005)

Clinton's and Blair's words are indeed not dissimilar from those pronounced by both George W. Bush and Nicolas Sarkozy a few years later. In the acceptance speech given in September 2004 for his second presidential candidacy, Bush said:

[A]nother priority for a new term is to build an ownership society, because ownership brings security, and dignity, and independence. Thanks to our policies homeownership in America is at an all-time high. (Bush, 2004)

In a similar vein, in 2006, French president Sarkozy declared:

As regards housing policy, my first priority is to turn France into a society of homeowners, because property favours the stability of the Republic, of Democracy and the Nation. (Sarkozy, 2006; author's translation; quoted in Philippe, 2006)

Within the space of three decades, the advent of neoliberalism had therefore revived long-standing views within capitalist countries that identified housing as the realm in which the ideal of a property-owning democracy materializes. With the precipitous reduction in the supply of public housing and the end or relaxation of rent regulation in many Western countries after the 'fiscal crisis of the state' in the 1960s and the 1970s (O'Connor, 1973), access to housing has increasingly taken the form of homeownership, granted by bank loans and involving growing household indebtedness. The expansion of mortgage markets and the consequent financialization of housing, therefore, have become distinguishing features of ascendant neoliberal capitalism and its crisis in the late 2000s. The advent of the financial crisis and the fact that it was clearly related to the mortgage default in the subprime sector led observers to question the sustainability of increasing rates of home-ownership obtained through the indebtedness of households within the middle and lower classes. The Financial Crisis Inquiry Report commissioned by the US Congress explicitly pointed the finger at the pernicious consequences of 'aggressive homeownership goals' (National Commission, 2011), while in September 2010 even the politically moderate *Time* magazine devoted the lead article on the front page to the theme: 'Rethinking homeownership. Why owning a home may no longer make economic sense' (Kiviat, 2010).

Just as the imperative of growth is rooted within US city politics, so the ideal of homeownership is ingrained in the US culture of capitalism and individual freedom. Government subsidy policies for homeownership, promoted by the newly established Federal Housing Administration, were a pillar of the New Deal embraced by President Franklin Delano Roosevelt in the 1930s, now commonly viewed as a paradigmatic example of Keynesianism. The 'American dream' evoked by both Clinton and Bush was built on this legacy, although this dream has turned into a nightmare following its fatal encounter with the financialized markets of the neoliberal era. However, even though the process of financialization during the neoliberal era has led to the bursting of the housing bubble, with destructive effects on the economy, contradictions that were intrinsic to a homeownership-based society were already apparent long before the neoliberal era, in what can be called the 'pre-histories of urban neoliberalism' (Aalbers, forthcoming). The Federal Housing Administration was created in 1934 with the aim of broadening access to homeownership amongst US social groups. but the pursuit of this goal has been systematically accompanied by the perpetuation of social discrimination and residential segregation in the housing market. The Community Reinvestment Act, approved in 1977 and subsequently reformed in the 1990s, was intended to tackle issues of discrimination and racial bias in the access to housing credit. Housing discrimination has historically affected African-Americans and Hispanics as banks denied them mortgages, particularly in so-called 'red-lined', undeserving neighbourhoods (Sugrue, 1996). That phenomenon has never disappeared despite official reassurances (Aalbers, 2011), and has re-emerged in even stronger forms after the financial crisis of the late 2000s, as recent red-lining lawsuits in cities like Buffalo, Newark and St Louis have shown (Swarns, 2015). The subprime mortgage schemes adopted since the 1990s, whose collapse was behind the financial crash of 2008, formalized this system of government-sponsored segregation, as this type of home loan became concentrated in urban neighbourhoods with high rates of low-income racial minorities. In the late 2000s, the bursting of the housing bubble had devastating effects, especially in large cities and metropolitan areas where the financialization of the built environment and the indebtedness of households were greater than elsewhere (Gotham, 2009).

In conclusion, as sites that condense phenomena of both social discrimination in the housing market and foreclosure of insolvent homeowners, contemporary cities are illustrative of the contradictions and nefarious consequences of the neoliberal appropriation of the capitalist culture of homeownership in a context marked by the centrality of the so-called secondary circuit of capital. Equally, as the next section will shown, socio-spatial inequalities are intimately linked to the dominant regime of societal governance, which turns urban creativity into a source of competition and socio-spatial differentiation at the same time.

NEOLIBERALIZING THE URBAN EXPERIENCE

The previous section of this chapter has shown how long-term distinctive features of capitalist cities, such as the imperative of growth, the relentless expansion of consumption and the cult of homeownership, have become key features of the neoliberal era, acquiring renewed centrality in contemporary capitalist cities. In this section, attention is directed to the reverse process: namely, how neoliberalism has subsumed within its rationality forms of societal phenomena that previously existed partially or fully outside the capitalist circuit of valorization in contemporary cities: urban creativity is a highly instructive example in this respect.

CREATIVE CITIES IN THE AGE OF INTEGRATED SPECTACLE

In his recently published 24/7: Late Capitalism and the Ends of Sleep, Jonathan Crary (2013) refers to Guy Debord's 'Comments on the Society of Spectacle' in which the Situationist theorist rereads his classic book which had appeared two decades earlier, arguing that contemporary societies were witnessing a shift from concentrated (typical of totalitarian regimes) and diffuse (typical of the American way of life) forms of spectacle which had prevailed in the 1960s, and which he analysed in La société du spectacle, to the current 'integrated society of spectacle' in which 'the spectacle has spread itself to the point where it now permeates all reality' (Debord, 1990: 9). This section, will provide evidence for the 'integrated society of spectacle' in the ways in which neoliberal cities – their politico-economic elites and the related machineries of government – have incorporated creativity into the value system of contemporary capitalist urbanism.

Creativity has a historically ambivalent relationship with capitalism, oscillating between incorporation on the one hand (from conventional technological innovation processes to today's post-Fordist knowledge-intensive industries) and autonomy or even opposition (creativity as transgression) on the other hand. Neoliberal urban regimes have attempted to neutralize this ambivalence, mobilizing powerful mechanisms of seduction of alternative subjectivities, for instance through the normalization of autonomous creative spaces and the spectacularization of social and cultural diversity (Coppola and Vanolo, 2015).

Creativity's process of appropriation into capitalism's cultural circuit has particularly intensified over the last two decades within the context of advanced liberal societies. An important contribution to this process has come from the publication of *The Rise of the Creative Class* in 2002, a best-selling book authored by Richard Florida, an economic geographer and urban planner at that time based in the deindustrializing city of Pittsburgh, in the middle of the US 'Rust Belt' (Florida, 2002). In this book, Florida has provided not only a new socio-cultural explanation but also a powerful narrative for what had already been identified by economic development scholars as the key role of technology and human capital as drivers of regional economic growth. In brief, Florida argues that the members of the creative class – notably, workers and professionals who make use of creative knowledge in their jobs, from architects and engineers to software developers, designers and other emerging figures in the information society – tend to favour urban environments characterized by the tolerance of socio-cultural diversity related to the presence of ethnic and sexual minorities as well as artistic communities. Moreover, according to Florida, creative-class members share values and attitudes based on ideas of meritocracy and individuality along with the willingness to be part of collaborative working environments.

Since its publication, Richard Florida's book has been enthusiastically welcomed by local politicians and economic elites, first in the USA, from which its empirical evidence was derived, and subsequently in a rapidly increasing number of 'wannabe' creative cities across the world. As a governmental technology enabling the cross-national mobility of urban development models, neoliberalism has allowed creativity to become a global narrative mobilized by policymakers and administrators in order to create consensus around newly proposed or already existing urban regeneration initiatives across the globe. While

Richard Florida in his book values initiatives designed to regenerate and preserve the historic background of cities, as well as to enhance their socio-cultural authenticity, social movements and critical observers lament the eradication of socio-cultural identity in the urban areas now attracting the creative class. In 2013, San Francisco – a city witnessing skyrocketing house prices in recent years – has seen longtime residents protesting against the unsustainable costs of living caused by the presence of the affluent creative professionals employed in Silicon Valley and residing in San Francisco (Steinmetz, 2014). On the other side, the so-called 'techies' and other newcomers have given rise to pro-market activist groups – such as the self-proclaimed San Francisco Bay Area Renters' Federation – demanding that local authorities increase the supply of housing by rolling back zoning regulations and environmental rules (Dougherty, 2016) – or the sort of political movement promoted by Airbnb, the home-sharing giant, in defence of 'the right to share' (Steinmetz, 2016a). These newly formed groups are in conflict with the traditional, left-leaning tenants' organizations, but are backed by real-estate developers and mainstream economists. These latter think that, in order to tackle the problem of soaring housing prices within tech-driven urban economies, rather than embracing traditionally progressive policies such as a housing policy based on investment in public and subsidized housing, or on rent-control legislation, city governments should resort to market-led 'smart growth policies' increasing the number of new housing units, thus keeping real-estate prices in check (Moretti, 2012).

In other contexts, the socio-spatial inequalities and the tensions associated in the USA with the post-recession tech boom arouse anger towards related cultural phenomena such as the hipster scene. In European cities, where the phenomenon is also particularly visible, recent times have seen periodical eruptions of social rage against the hipster. In Berlin a group called *Hipster Antifa Neukölln* has attracted media attention, with its protests against soaring rents caused by

tourists and hipsters in Neukölln (Stallwood, 2012). This neighbourhood has been more mildly touched by gentrification processes compared with fast-gentrifying areas in Berlin, such as Prenzelauer Berg
and Kreuzbeurg, which were once strongholds of alternative cultural
and political movements. In London anti-gentrification radical activists have violently attacked a cereal café in Shoreditch (Khomami
and Halliday, 2015), an ex-working-class area in East London, which
became a model for creative urban regeneration in the 1990s and is
now associated with the booming high-tech economy (Nathan and
Vandore, 2014). But in other contexts, such as in the fast-growing
city of Shenzhen, in south-eastern China, hipsters, artists and techies
are part of the community of city dwellers – mostly composed of
immigrants of rural origin – in informal settlements, facing demolition
plans pursued by the national government in order to make way for
new skyscraper complexes (Feng, 2016).

In Western cities, however, this presence is undoubtedly associated with processes of gentrification and the eradication of local identity, especially in historic neighbourhoods. In a recent study, Richard
Florida and his fellow researchers have recognized the fact that in
economically dynamic cities such as Chicago, Washington, Boston
and New York, the creative class's colonization of downtown districts
forces service and working-class residents to relocate outside of the
central city to the least desirable parts of town, leading to novel forms
of socio-spatial segregation (Florida et al., 2014). However, in this
study, as well as in a new section entitled 'Contradictions' which he has
added to the revised edition of *The Rise of the Creative Class* (2012),
Florida does not provide detailed policy solutions to this problem,
even though he writes that: 'real opportunities must be provided for
all residents, so that rewards and promises of the creative city can be
shared more equally' (2012: 370). In the conclusion, he evokes a 'creative compact' replacing the Keynesian social compact of the second
post-war decades, with the aim of addressing the new socio-spatial

inequalities and demands for economic growth arising from the transformations of contemporary capitalism:

> The creative compact would be dedicated to the *creatification* of everyone. It would expand participation in the Creative Economy to industrial and service workers, leverage new private and public investment in human infrastructure, innovation, education, and our cities, while reaffirming and maintaining America's long-held commitment to diversity. It would restructure education, moving away from rote learning and overly bureaucratic schools and creativity-squelching standards. It would set in place a new social safety net that invests in people and provides mobile benefits that follow workers from job to job. It would recast urban policy as a cornerstone of economic policy and ensure that America remains a beacon for the best, brightest, most energetic and ambitious people in the world. (Florida, 2012: 385)

According to Florida, the 'creative compact' should be centred on three spheres: (1) education and human capital; (2) professional training; and (3) urban policy. As regards the latter, in this part of the book he does not offer details about what kind of 'urban policy' he envisages. To find details of urban policy, one has to look at the concluding chapter of part four ('Community'), entitled 'Building the Creative Community'. The proper discussion of policy ideas in this chapter is preceded by the elucidation of the idea that the USA, as well as other advanced economies, is witnessing the rise of what he calls the 'urban tech' (Ibid: 322): the fact that cities like San Francisco and Seattle in the USA, and London and Berlin in Europe, are giving rise to innovative technology districts based on start-up firms, thus becoming new centres of production and innovation, challenging the traditional suburban pattern of the tech industry epitomized by Silicon Valley. Cities have, therefore, gained a new centrality within the geographies of capitalism, as discussed earlier in this book (chapters 1 and 2). However, it is in the last section of the present chapter that readers can discern the kind of urban policy that Florida advocates. Rather than presenting a detailed policy framework, he draws his ideas from evidence obtained from four cases of urban economic development: Austin, Dublin, Las Vegas and Pittsburgh.

In the short introduction to this case-study analysis, Florida premises his discussion on the idea that in order to build a creative community we need to avoid initiatives 'from the top down', privileging instead 'smart strategies that recognize and enhance bottom-up, community-based efforts that are already working' (Ibid: 349). He thus brings together, in an evocative manner, the contemporary notion of 'smart strategies' – derived from the urban tech culture – and the idea of the 'bottom-up' and 'community-based', two terms evoking progressive traditions of advocacy and participatory planning in the 1960s and the 1970s (Sites, 2010). The original aim of progressive urbanism was to empower urban communities by addressing the needs of deprived neighbourhoods, low-income residents and disadvantaged ethnic minorities. However, looking at the evidence that Florida draws from his four case studies, there is no sign of progressive planning. Rather, there is the proposal of a 'thin policy' (Peck, 2001), based on a set of recommendations reflecting a conventionally neoliberal rationale of fiscal incentives, small government and corporatism, supplemented by measures aimed at improving the attractiveness of urban environments in terms of culture and lifestyle (elaborated by him in an earlier chapter of his book as being 'abundant high quality amenities and experiences, an openness to diversity of all kinds' (Florida, 2012: 186)). Referring to the case of Austin, a city that has become a recognized hub for the high-tech economy in the past few decades, Florida emphasizes two aspects: first, the fact that 'the city's leadership made benchmarking visits to leading high-tech regions'; second, that 'the region has made considerable investments in its lifestyle and music scene' (Ibid: 340). Moreover, according to Florida, the case of Dublin – a city that has left behind years of industrial decline and emigration, becoming home for leading US multinationals in the

ITC sector such as IBM and Microsoft – shows the importance of an expansionary fiscal policy based on the alleviation of the tax base, along with the revitalization of the urban environment, as Florida draws attention to the 'financial and tax-related incentives' that 'helped attract high-tech giants', as well as 'the tax breaks' offered to 'culturally creative people' such as musicians and writers, and a 'high-quality place to live and work' (Ibid: 341–2). The third case study, which deals with Las Vegas, is also instructive, as Florida refers to this city as an example of 'corporate neo-urbanism' (Ibid: 345), where Zappos, a successful digital company selling shoes online (now acquired by Amazon), and led by visionary CEO Tony Hsieh, has moved its headquarters into the inner city, revitalizing the 'struggling downtown core'. In this context, the company's CEO has taken the lead in the ambitious 'Downtown Project' aimed at producing ' "collisions" between people – facilitate relationships and spark ideas' (Ibid: 344). Florida concludes his recounting of the Las Vegas case, proposing it as a 'new model', 'an interesting and important experiment that may point the way to the revitalization of many other struggling downtown urban centers' (Ibid: 345). Finally, the case of Pittsburgh (entitled 'still the base case', as this was his hometown when he wrote the first edition of his book) shows the improvements made during the previous decade as the city has embarked on a relatively successful path of urban transformation centred on the stimulation of the high-tech economy, the revitalization of the urban cultural scene and the preservation of its historic centre. Pittsburgh, however, as Florida acknowledges, is still depopulated compared with the post-war Fordist era and is also predominantly white. As an ethnically (and socially) cleansed city, Pittsburgh, therefore, cannot provide evidence of the 'contradictions' mentioned by Florida in the title of this part of the book. Its conventional image is rather that of a 'poster child for managing industrial transition', according to a representative of local area developers, as the city's Wikipedia page emphasizes.

The 'creative compact' theorized by Richard Florida and embraced by several city governments across the world derives its popularity from the fact of bringing together such diverse urban communities and related interests as artists, professionals and high-tech companies (both early-stage and established), as well as of offering a politico-economic discourse that is at one and the same time attentive to the imperative of economic growth and sensitive to its contradictions in the form of socio-spatial inequalities. However, as said above, Florida does not indicate the way in which these inequalities and contradictions can be actually resolved or at least reduced in their social impact, offering instead a policy rationale based on conventionally neoliberal economic policy prescriptions and a narrow set of reassuring examples. The worldwide success of Florida's theory of the creative class and its transmutation into subsequent theorizations of smart and start-up urbanism is illustrative of the age of 'integrated spectacle' identified by Guy Debord. This age of integrated spectacle is only partly based on events, festivals, exhibitions and other visible forms of spectacularized city life. Such manifestations of the integrated society of spectacle are important, but they tell us only part of the story. The whole story of the contemporary capitalist city tells us that any form of life producing knowledge, affects and economies of invention is potentially subsumed within the hegemonic projects of urban regeneration embraced under the rubric of creative and, more recently, smart urbanism.

CONCLUSION

This chapter has looked at the two-sided relationship of neoliberalism with the urban phenomenon. In particular, it appears there has been a continuity in the mutual reinforcement between cities and neoliberalism up to the current global age, showing their relationship of immanence with global capitalism. This means that neoliberalism has incorporated long-term features of social life within capitalist cities, such as the relentless expansion of consumption and the commodification of housing. During the so-called golden age of capitalism, the Keynesian mode of economic regulation temporarily mitigated processes of commodification, which neoliberalism has subsequently revived. At the same time, neoliberalism is not only drawing on pre-existing characteristic features of capitalist urbanization, but has also expanded the economic base of contemporary cities, incorporating societal phenomena that previously existed partially or fully outside the capitalist circuit of valorization, such as creativity.

This two-sided relationship of mutual reinforcement explains the key contribution of critical urban studies to the understanding of contemporary neoliberalism. It is likely that ongoing processes of global urbanization, with the geographical extension of urbanization processes and related neoliberalization dynamics spreading across the globalized world, will not only intensify the intimate relationship between cities and neoliberalism but will also bring to light other aspects in which this relationship takes shape. Moreover, this mutuality is not limited to the described relationship between cities and neoliberalism. Cities are sources of crisis and austerity but also of promised resurgence for contemporary capitalism, as the latest global economic crisis has demonstrated; a crisis with clear urban roots, owing to the unprecedented financialization of housing markets that has particularly affected indebted households living in large cities and metropolitan areas. On the one hand, during the crisis, cities have been key sites for the implementation of austerity measures adopted in compliance with the fiscal consolidation targets imposed by international financial institutions and national governments to municipalities and regional administrations. On the other hand, cities are key spaces of resurgence for capitalist economies, as urban environments concentrate the 'commonwealth' of contemporary societies. Chapter 5 will show how this dual role of cities in macroeconomic terms is reflected in the fluctuating forms of life that characterize contemporary urban societies.

4 Diffusions

The previous chapters of this book have shown how the dominant phenomena of our times, such as globalization and neoliberalism, have intimate relationships to cities, understood as urban societies, economies and political entities. With regard to globalization, chapter 2 has examined how urban scholarship has conceptualized the role of cities in the process of globalization through territorial, networked and relational lenses. With regard to neoliberalism, chapter 3 has laid emphasis on the process of cross-fertilization, as cities and neoliberalism have borrowed key elements from each other, leading to a close association which is customarily labelled 'urban neoliberalism' or 'neoliberal urbanism', and which has resulted in serious consequences following the financial collapse of 2008.

The present chapter offers an interpretation of the global geographies of contemporary capitalism from an urban perspective, viewing the defining feature of the process of globalization and neoliberalization, particularly in its constitutive stages (in the late 1980s and the early 1990s), as the production and diffusion of a 'one-dimensional city', based on forms of mass consumption derived from dominant Western cultures and especially those of the American lifestyle. As in Torsten Hägerstrand's theory of innovation, the notion of diffusion presupposes the existence of a centre from which the first appearance of a social form develops and spreads, to impose itself elsewhere until a saturation point is reached (Hägerstrand, 1967). This chapter will consider how the diffusion of a 'one-dimensional city' originating in the West, and particularly in the USA, is a defining characteristic of global urbanization, and how this has laid the foundation for global experimenting with a neoliberal logic of societal governance and urban management: a 'civilizing process' – understood as a 'general impulsion towards economic monopolization' of human experience (Elias, 2000: 306) – of human behaviour and forms of societal governance, brought about by these forces in a context of globalizing capitalist urbanization.

However, drawing on postcolonial insights within urban scholarship, the chapter will also go beyond a centripetal view of homogenization, underscoring the need to embrace a place-sensitive approach in order to understand the geographical-historical articulations of these diffusion processes, calling attention to the particularities of societal contexts and the temporalities of capitalist globalization.

ONE-DIMENSIONAL CITY

In the 1960s, Herbert Marcuse famously theorized the way in which advanced capitalist societies impose a one-dimensional way of thinking and living through technology and mass consumption, drawing a veil over the contradictions of capitalism and its inherently revolutionary potential, by giving citizens the illusion of freedom and spiritual satisfaction from the consumption of commodities (Marcuse, 1991). The book's opening sentence – 'a comfortable, smooth, reasonable, democratic unfreedom prevails in advanced industrial civilization, a token of technical progress' (Ibid: 3) – soon became a classic in twentieth-century critical theory. Four decades earlier, combining Weber's theory of rationalization with Marx's concept of commodity fetishism, György Lukács had proposed the theory of reification, understood as a process involving the totality of social realms (Lukács, 1999; see chapter 3). Lukács' work has been a source of inspiration for Theodor Adorno's theorization of exchange value as the organizing principle of advanced capitalist economies: a forced universalization of the human experience obliterating the very possibility of difference (Adorno, 2004; see chapter 3). Along related lines, writing together with Max Horkheimer, another key exponent of the Frankfurt School, Adorno coined the famous notion of 'culture industry', which posits that artwork ineluctably becomes subjected to the laws of the market economy within late capitalist societies (Adorno and Horkheimer, 2002).

Social scientists dealing with the incipient globalization of social life in the early 1990s, particularly those concentrating on the expansion of consumer culture in post-industrial societies, re-evaluated the Frankfurt School and related authors like Lukács, whose work had been stigmatized as elitist and even totalitarian by the anti-Marxist proponents of the postmodern turn, such as the so-called 'new philosophers' in France in the late 1970s (such as André Glucksmann and Bernard-Henri Lévy) and the hermeneutical advocates of 'weak thought' in Italy in the early 1980s (whose leading figure was Gianni Vattimo, who later rediscovered Marxism: Vattimo and Zabala, 2011). Sociologists and critical theorists investigating globalization in the 1990s not only looked at the centrality attributed to the phenomenon of omnivore consumption and commodification within the Frankfurt School, but were also interested in the attention devoted by those thinkers to the sense of totalizing social order, which they now associated with hegemonic narratives of postmodernity and the global age (Featherstone, 1991). From this perspective, a decisive theoretical contribution came from Frederic Jameson, who reinterpreted postmodernism as a specific stage of 'late capitalism', a term he borrowed from Adorno and from Marxist economist Ernest Mandel, characterized by the 'cultural dominant' (Jameson, 1991). In a more sociological vein, drawing inspiration from Marcuse's thesis, Leslie Sklair signalled the transformation of the 'culture-ideology of consumerism' 'from a sectional preference of the rich to a globalizing phenomenon', enabled by a global system of mass media and the adoption of the shopping mall as a customary site of consumption in the most disparate corners of the world (Sklair, 1991).

It is in this context that the phenomena of McDonaldization, Disneyfication, and Guggenheimization came to symbolize the early stages of globalization in the 1990s. It was thought that these forces were leading to a process of societal homogenization of increasingly urbanized societies across the world. As noted in chapter 2, this idea was powerfully reinforced by the diffusion of mass consumption that resulted from global urbanization in emerging neo-capitalist econo-mies. The process of homogenization, therefore, was understood as a consequence of both widespread market-oriented economic reform around the world, commonly associated with the 'global shift' (Dicken, 2011), and the standardization of lifestyles, particularly of the sphere of consumption, due to the geographical expansion of capitalist urbani-zation. While the present chapter provides an analysis of the geo-graphical diffusion of the colonizing forces, the following chapter will show how the neoliberal logic of governmentality goes beyond that, its ultimate goal being the entrepreneurialization of society and the self as a way of reconciling itself with the configuration of contemporary capitalism – a configuration that is based on the economic valorization of socially diffused knowledge.

The homogenization effects are those more conventionally associ-ated with the incessant globalization of economies and societies since the end of the Cold War era in the late 1980s. Common wisdom has long held the idea that globalization has led to a uniformity of forms of production, consumption and social life in the contemporary world. There is strong evidence to support this 'common-sense' view, which in many respects is hard to refute. It is, in other words, a self-evident 'truth', as the defining feature of contemporary globalization is the fact that we consume tangible and intangible goods that are increasingly uniform across the planet. This process is fostered by the circulation of goods and information enabled by both tangible and intangible technologies, such as the shipping container (Levinson, 2006) and the Internet. When opinion-makers and the mass media have commented on the effects of the late 2000s economic downturn, the commonly held view has been to associate the slowdown of globalization with a diminished degree of market interconnectedness as measured by the movement of goods and services (*The Economist*, 2009; Gross, 2009).

The idea of globalization as a homogenizing force was prevalent in the early stages of this phenomenon, when it was seen as a force deeply shaping human experience in totalizing forms, a view that still dominates representations within the wider public. Different phenomena have brought to light this idea of homogenization, but the most influential can be considered those of McDonaldization, Disneyfication and Guggenheimization. In all these phenomena, urban environments have played a key role, not merely as containers of predetermined societal phenomena but as places that are constitutive of globalizing social relations. Without cities and their outer spaces, globalization could not exist or develop its potential, as urban settings offer a multiplier effect generated by the coexistence of specialization and diversity economies (see chapter 2). At the same time, emphasis on the particularities of place-based institutional arrangements and socio-historical contexts helps us convey a more nuanced understanding of cultural homogenization processes and their limits.

MCDONALDIZATION AND THE RISE OF CAPITALIST GLOBALIZATION

The general public started becoming aware of the advent of globalization in the early 1990s, following the dissolution of the Soviet Union and the end of the Cold War era that was centred on the opposition between capitalism and socialism. At this stage, there was a perception that the capitalist logic of wealth accumulation and goods consumption was bound to prevail throughout the world (at least in the urbanized world), making non-capitalist forms of societal organization residual or statistically irrelevant. Socialist economies appeared confined to a few remaining enclaves such as China, Cuba, Laos, Vietnam and North Korea. Of these, China and Vietnam – the most significant in terms of population and economic power – had also embarked on market-oriented reform, which will be discussed here with reference to the former. In this historical context, the public's attention became captured by the spectacle of an upcoming era of global consumption. This revelation was powerfully represented by the large crowds waiting in line for admission to the newly opened McDonald's restaurants in Moscow in 1990, and in Beijing in 1992.

McDonald's opening in the central Pushkin Square in Moscow is documented by a handful of short films still available on video-sharing websites, showing endless queues of customers patiently waiting outside the restaurant amidst winter's freezing temperatures. This opening was part of Soviet president Gorbachev's strategy to ensure a greater freedom by opening the country to external relations and forms of market economy (the so-called *perestroika*). In a way, the acceptance of McDonald's was the Soviet regime's attempt to satisfy people's eagerness for capitalism, which had remained frustrated in previous years despite the expectations linked to *perestroika*. However, the attempt proved to be in vain as the Soviet Union collapsed only a year later, in 1991. At the time of Gorbachev, a more open atti-tude towards fashion culture had also started gaining ground amongst the Communist Party's elites, but in real life things had not changed much for ordinary people, who could find only a limited number of Western clothes in second-hand shops and through informal chan-nels (Bartlett, 2010). The arrival of McDonald's thus remained an exception, partly due to the determination of the American corpo-ration, which negotiated for fourteen years with Soviet authorities to open the Pushkin Square restaurant, the negotiations themselves being officially conducted by McDonald's Canada, to avoid the Cold War's anti-US prejudice. In the following years, McDonald's steadily expanded its presence in Russia, establishing itself also in small towns. However, despite the process of domestication and incorporation into Russia's food and wider consumer culture (Caldwell, 2004), in recent years McDonald's has partially lost its popularity due to the new wave of anti-Americanism within the Russian public realm. In 2014, after sanitary inspections, its flagship restaurant in Pushkin Square had to close down due to supposed hygiene violations, and its subsequent reopening drew criticism from nationalist parties (Amos, 2014).

While in Russia McDonald's played a pioneering role in the spread of Western consumer culture, in China its arrival was preceded by that of another US fast-food giant, Kentucky Fried Chicken. The latter opened a restaurant in Beijing in November 1987, in a street adjacent to Tiananmen Square, and attracted a huge inflow of consumers. The opening of KFC has to be understood against the background of the process of economic reform in China which had been embraced by Deng Xiaoping since the late 1970s. This process was explicitly aimed at the attraction of foreign trade and investment, but was not accompanied by political reform, thus laying the foundations for the Chinese variety of capitalism which is commonly understood as 'state capitalism' or 'socialist market economy' (Peck and Zhang, 2013). The creation of about twenty special economic zones in cities along the coast where international investors received favourable tariff and tax treatment became the flagship policy in this strategy at the macroeconomic level. The economic reform process had a strong impact on urban lifestyles, leading to the early stages of the consumer revolution in China in the late 1980s (see chapter 2), something that in Russia was far from happening. Susan Shirk, in the introduction to her book on China's economic reform, offers a fascinating comparative account of the urban contexts in Russia and China at that time:

In the fall of 1991 I visited China and Russia. Urban economic conditions in the two countries presented a striking contrast. The streets of Chinese cities were bustling with commercial activity. Shoppers thronged private and collective shops displaying the latest Hong Kong fashions manufactured in China. Couples debated whether to spend their savings on microwave ovens or tape recorders. Doting parents purchased Japanese electronic keyboards for their children. Market counters displayed an abundance of vegetables, fruit, meat, and seafood [...]. Conditions in Russian cities were much bleaker. Compared with China, the number of private or collective businesses was infinitesimal and their supply of consumer goods meager. People stood in line for hours, and when they finally made it inside the shops, they found little to buy. The shelves of state stores were even barer. Basic foods were in short supply, especially in Moscow. Sugar and cheese were impossible to find and eggs almost as scarce, even in private markets. (Shirk, 1993: 3)

Shirk's account shows the importance of urban societal contexts, which can be compared with that of macroeconomic policies and governance structures. The fast-food sector was not the only Western-oriented consumer revolution in Chinese cities, as international fashion and clothing stores started appearing in Beijing and Shanghai from the late 1980s onwards (Croll, 2006). However, the fast-food sector played an even stronger role in this consumer revolution. In particular, the arrival and spread of McDonald's in the early 1990s introduced substantial changes to the food habits of Chinese consumers, as hamburgers were previously unknown in this country, while the fried chicken meals sold by KFC were similar to traditional Chinese food. By 1996, within the space of four years, McDonald's had opened twenty-nine restaurants in Beijing alone. McDonald's offered consumers not just hamburgers and French fries, but also a comfortable eating environment, with specific sections dedicated to children and romantic couples (Yan, 2006). As in Russia, in recent times Western fast-food chains have seen their sales declining in China: KFC has been hit by scandals linked to the alleged use of antiviral drugs in chickenfeed; McDonald's is afflicted by changing consumption patterns in this country, reflecting a more global trend which sees the rising phenomenon of 'fast-casual dining', centred on allegedly healthier, ethnically diverse food gaining ground at the expense of conventional fast-food chains.

In the 1990s, the role played by McDonald's and similar chain restaurants in the Westernization of urban societies in Russia, China and almost everywhere in the globalizing world offered a powerful demonstration of the thesis of the McDonaldization of contemporary societies, which had been proposed a few years earlier with reference to the North American context (Ritzer, 1983). According to this thesis, the adoption of the 'McDonald's model' has a rationalizing effect on contemporary societies in a Weberian sense. In the early twentieth century, the great German sociologist famously theorized the relationship between Protestantism and the ascendancy of capitalism in light of the key contribution provided by its work ethic to the rationalization of industrialized societies, which made societies uniform in their functioning, turning them into governable entities (Weber, 2001). Similarly, the phenomenon of global McDonald's became illustrative of the tendency to make social processes efficient, foreseeable and measurable. In 1986, *The Economist* coined the so-called Big Mac Index in order to compare purchasing power in different currencies, thus turning McDonald's commodity into a general equivalent of the capitalist economy, given its 'socially validated monopoly of equivalence', to put it in Marxian terms (De Brunhoff, 1976: 23). The automation of labour in the service sector, enabled by technological advances and the extension of the assembly line outside the factory walls, provided the socio-technical base for this process of rationalization within increasingly post-industrial and globalizing societies.

Subsequent developments have confirmed the scenario of McDonaldization, understood as a process of homogenization of consumer culture in capitalist societies. This has occurred in two different ways. On the one hand, the fact of customers waiting in line to purchase especially desired goods has become a ritual in contemporary capitalist societies: in January 2014, the BBC broadcast a short documentary interviewing people queuing to buy a new iPhone model in Regent Street, London (some of them for three entire days). Similar scenes are now customary in capitalist cities across the world: in Italian cities, people queue to buy the latest model of the expensive Hogan shoes even in times of economic recession when the majority of shops are suffering. In August 2011, London saw compulsive consumerism turning into social rage when angry youngsters from minority backgrounds, mostly living in underserved areas on the outskirts, looted shops and megastores, particularly targeting mobile phones. This rage was triggered by the death of a young man shot by police in Tottenham, North London, a multi-ethnic area with the highest unemployment rate at the city level. On the other hand, even the phenomenon of sustainable food undergoes a process of commodified homogenization, particularly in the affluent societies of the West. As noticed above, the rise of fast-casual chain restaurants, offering supposedly healthier and culturally diverse food, is just another form of consumerism. But the same can be said with reference to sustainable food being sold in large-scale retail stores such as supermarkets, as argued by Raj Patel in his *Stuffed and Starved* book:

> While there is an important environmental difference between industrially produced organic food and industrially produced non-organic food [...], the social difference between industrially produced organic and non-organic food at the supermarket is vanishingly small. (Patel, 2007: 246)

In the USA, the other side of the coin of the gentrification of urban supermarkets in the affluent areas is the deliberate disinvestment of supermarket chains in the most deprived neighbourhoods, particularly those inhabited by African-Americans and Hispanics, a phenomenon known as 'supermarket red-lining', leading to the rise of so-called 'food deserts', particularly in industrially declining and demographically shrinking cities in the 'Rustbelt' (Eisenhauer, 2001). This phenomenon reproduces the same logic underlying red-lining practices historically adopted by financial institutions in the housing market in the USA and elsewhere.

In the affluent areas, however, the globalization of sustainable food consumption and the related lifestyles is not confined to large-scale retail stores but also affects small shops adopting the philosophy of slow and local food: artisan gelato makers, bio restaurants and cafés, ethnic grocery stores and a variety of rustic eateries are proliferating in contemporary cities, particularly in the fast-gentrifying neighbourhoods inhabited by members of the 'creative class' (see chapter 3). This phenomenon is an example of the reinvention of authenticity as an engine, at one and the same time, of urban economic growth and further socio-spatial differentiation. As Sharon Zukin points out: 'during the past thirty years, food has emerged as the new "art" in the urban cultural experience' (Zukin, 2010: 29), becoming a key ingredient for urban 'authenticity': 'a tool, along with economic and political power, to control not just the look but the use of real urban places: neighbourhoods, parks, community gardens, shopping streets' (Ibid: xiii). In a subsequent article, Sharon Zukin and her colleagues have explored the role played by the so-called 'discursive investors' in urban gentrification, analysing the reviews of restaurants on a popular website in the USA (Yelp, based in San Francisco, one of the leading companies of the Web 2.0 generation) that promotes 'trendy' restaurants, shedding a negative light on more traditional eating places favoured by long-term residents (Zukin et al., 2015).

This phenomenon of discursive production of gentrification reflects the increasingly blurred boundaries between production and consumption within contemporary 'experience economies'. These economies are deeply influenced by online communication and the ever-increasing amount of user-generated content: a phenomenon that has led George Ritzer – the original proponent of the McDonaldization thesis – and Nathan Jurgenson to coin the notion of 'prosumer capitalism' (Ritzer and Jurgenson, 2010). In a previous article, Jurgenson argued that the advent of Web 2.0 has led to a de-McDonaldization of the Internet, with respect to distinctive features of McDonaldization identified by Ritzer such as calculability, efficiency, predictability and control through digital technologies, which now have to coexist with the explosive character of user-generated content (Jurgenson, 2010).

In Marxian terms, this phenomenon and the wider experience of so-called 'prosumer capitalism' is symptomatic of the changing dynamic of 'real abstraction' at a time of post-Fordist, cognitive capitalism. As Alberto Toscano points out, in modern capitalist societies the monetary commensuration of commodity values hides the secret of 'real abstraction' intrinsic in commodity exchange; as Slavoj Žižek puts it: 'in the act of exchange the commodity is reduced to an abstract entity which – irrespective of its particular nature, of its "use value" – possesses "the same value" as another commodity for which it is being exchanged' (Žižek, 2008: 10–11). Thus, in post-Fordist, knowledge-intensive capitalism the process of real abstraction involves forms of life (knowledge, affects, communicational skills) embodied in the general intellect, which has become a productive force per se (Toscano, 2008). These points need to be borne in mind when interpreting the shift from the McDonaldization era, in which McDonald's was identified as a general equivalent of commodity exchange (epitomized by the Big Mac Index), to the current post-McDonaldization phase, characterized by an inherent tension between the persisting forms of control and rationalization pursued by multinational corporations and the general intellect that is incorporated in the phenomenon of 'prosumer' economies.

DISNEYFICATION AND THE SPATIO-TEMPORAL
MORATORIUM OF LATE CAPITALISM

In the early 1990s, the Disneyfication thesis acquired particular relevance within scholarship dealing with the postmodernization of the urban experience, emphasizing aspects of deterritorialization and the shaping of a centre-less urban form, and particularly illustrated by Los Angeles as a paradigmatic expression of postmodern urbanism (Dear and Flusty, 1998) and urbanization (Soja, 2000). In this context, Disneyfication was seen as the synthesis of more general trends leading cities to become entertainment machines and centres of mass consumption – open-air theme parks in which the experience of leisure time becomes spectacularized in an increasing number of geographical settings across the world. In the words of a key article entitled 'See you in Disneyland', written by urbanist Michael Sorkin:

> Disney World, a theme park of theme parks, is America's stand-in for Elysium, the ultimate reward for quarterbacks and pitchers, the utopia of leisure. And it's not just America's: through those pearly gates in Orlando, Florida, lies the leading purely tourist destination on the planet, welcoming close to 100,000 people on good days, over thirty million a year, a throng that spends nearly a billion dollars each year. These staggering numbers include neither the original Disneyland in Anaheim, California, nor Tokyo Disneyland, nor Euro-Disneyland, a building by the Marne. Thanks to Disney and like attractions, Orlando has become America's capital of transience, with more hotel rooms than Chicago, Los Angeles, or New York. (Sorkin, 1992: 5)

In the eyes of urbanists and social scientists writing in the 1990s, Disney appeared as the most powerful manifestation of the society of spectacle theorized by Guy Debord in the late 1960s. As noted in chapter 3, in the late 1980s Debord had revised his notion of society of spectacle by adding the idea of 'integration' in relation to the advent of post-Fordist economies at that time, as opposed to the concentrated and diffuse forms of spectacle prevailing in Fordist times. Chapter 3 accepted Debord's conceptualization, particularly linking the idea of integrated society of spectacle with the incorporation of urban creativity into the capitalist mode of production. As Disney resorts precede post-Fordist economies, even though their development has continued in a context of post-Fordism, it can be argued that, rather than representing a paradigmatic manifestation of postmodernism as Michael Sorkin and others have perhaps too hastily maintained, Disneyfication represents a persistence of 'late capitalism' characterized by concentrated forms of spectacle within contemporary societies, univocally derived from one dominant cultural source, i.e., the so-called 'American way of life'. This argument is not intended to downplay the current relevance of the Disneyfication phenomenon, with the unprecedented popularity of Disney characters in recent times, such as the so-called 'Frozen-mania'. Rather, the aim here is to identify a continuity between the era of 'late capitalism' preceding the advent of globalization as a discursive phenomenon, where cultural domination was practised in colonizing forms reflecting the imperialist strategies pursued by the nation-states, and that of neoliberal globalizing societies characterized by boundless, networked forms of power and governance (Hardt and Negri, 2000: 166). At the same time, as this chapter will show, Disneyland – particularly its localization in Orlando, Florida, evoked by Sorkin – anticipates (in a context of late Keynesianism) the neoliberalization of urban and regional development, which will become generalized in the following decades across the world.

While theorists of global governance and the Empire, such as Michael Hardt and Antonio Negri, consider the changing forms of governance of contemporary capitalism in terms of 'passages of sovereignty', emphasis here is on the juxtaposition of pre-extant and novel forms with related socio-spatial patterns of governance and cultural domination, in which the diffusion of Western colonizing forces coexists with advanced forms of neoliberalization in urban societies. Walt Disney is a significant example of the former as defined in the introduction to this chapter, as it still embodies a distinctively American form of cultural domination. Having been founded in the 1920s, Walt Disney has become an icon of US capitalism and the related corporate culture throughout the twentieth century and beyond. Along with its popular movies and cartoons, Disney's worldwide fame is firmly linked to its theme parks. Disney resorts are amusement parks in which visitors can find a variety of recreational attractions, along with restaurants, hotels and associated facilities for both employees and visitors. Disney parks and resorts originally appeared in the USA and then spread in cities (more precisely, in their neighbouring suburban areas) across the world: in chronological order, Los Angeles, Orlando, Tokyo, Paris, Hong Kong, Shanghai. Not only the geographical distribution but also the temporal succession of Disney parks deserves attention, as it reflects the changing geographies of contemporary capitalism from the post-Second World War era onwards. As an iconic expression of post-war American capitalism, this section shows how the expansion of Disney in the 'new world' of globalization is illustrative of a spatio-temporal moratorium of late capitalism, rather than a paradigmatic manifestation of postmodern urbanism, as urban theorists held in the early 1990s. The use of the term 'spatio-temporal moratorium' draws inspiration from developmental psychologist Erik Erikson, who wrote about the 'psychosocial moratorium' of late adolescents, understood as a 'prolongation of the interval between youth and adulthood' (Erikson, 1994: 143).

The first Walt Disney amusement park appeared in 1955 in the USA, in California, in the city of Anaheim, in the Orange County and in the metropolitan area of Los Angeles, and was followed by a subsequent project at Lake Buena Vista, near Orlando, Florida, finalized in 1971. Disney's selection of these sites is highly significant, as they are both located within the core of the so-called Sunbelt (the vast region stretching across the southeast and the southwest), the new frontier of capitalist development in the USA after the decline of the old industrialized regions of the 'Frostbelt' (in the northeast and the midwest), which subsequently became known as the 'Rustbelt', specializing in heavy industries associated with the Fordist era. The notion of 'Sunbelt' was coined in 1969 by a Republican strategist named Kevin Philips, in order to identify a large region in the south of the USA touching twelve states, including southern California and Florida, characterized by suburban development and the dominance of conservative values (Tandy Shermer, 2011). In the 1960s and the 1970s, following the social welfare programmes that had been pursued within the framework of Roosevelt's New Deal from the 1930s onwards, the south witnessed intense economic growth due to Federal defence programmes, which helped to establish the region as national leader in aerospace, electronics and 'business climate' (Schulman, 1991). This reveals the central role played by the 'entrepreneurial state' in the rise of what is customarily known as the post-Fordist Sunbelt, bringing together a Schumpeterian emphasis on technological innovation as a motor of economic growth with a demand-driven, Keynesian approach to economic development (Eisinger, 1988). In this context, Orange County – where Disneyland was first created – represented a highly significant context in both spatial and economic terms: an example at the same time of 'post-suburban spatial formation' – a multicentred, ethnically diverse metropolitan region combining residential, commercial and productive functions (Kling et al., 1991) – and of a high-technology industrial complex in the Sunbelt, alongside the Silicon Valley in California, the Dallas–Fort Worth area in Texas and the Research Triangle Park in North Carolina (Scott, 1988).

However, despite its economic strength, the Californian Orange County and the city of Anaheim more particularly, with its congested urban growth, never entirely satisfied Walt Disney, the patron and founding father of the company, who was in search of a greenfield site where he could plan and realize a 'city of tomorrow' (Foglesong, 2001). Orlando and its surroundings looked suited for this purpose, as the area was still underpopulated and mainly agricultural. In 1966, Disney easily obtained from the Florida State legislature an Act authorizing the creation of the 'Reedy Creek Improvement District' (named after a natural waterway), which is still operating: a 'special taxing district' acting with the same authority and responsibility as a county government, in which 'Walt Disney World accounts for 85 per cent of the revenues collected', as the official website reports (<www.rcid.org>). Thanks to Disney World, Orlando has become one of the most popular tourist destinations in the world and amongst the fastest-growing urban regions in the USA in terms of population and wealth (its population has more than doubled over the last four decades, shifting from almost 100,000 in 1970 to 230,000 in 2010), thus becoming a model for the privatization of societal government and the deregulation of land use. In the following decades, while cities in Florida have been characterized by the adoption of a markedly pro-growth agenda (Turner, 1992), business improvement districts have become a prominent example of mobile policy of urban development in neoliberal times, having been transferred from North America to a number of countries across the world (Ward, 2006).

The success achieved with the original model of Disneyland in California and its first reproduction in Florida induced Walt Disney to go international, founding a new resort outside the USA about every decade from the 1980s onwards. The first step was the opening of Tokyo Disneyland in 1983. This was followed by Euro Disney in Paris (subsequently renamed Disneyland Paris) in 1992, by Hong Kong in 2005 and finally by Shanghai, which opened in June 2016. In all cases, except for Tokyo where the resort is owned and wholly operated by a Japanese firm, Walt Disney Company shares the ownership with local public and private investors. However, in both physical and socio-cultural terms, the overseas resorts intentionally reproduce, even duplicate, the original American model of Disneyland. This happens even when place-specific details have been added, as in the case of Tokyo (Van Maanen, 1992), within an inevitable process of adaptation to local culture and land-use regulations. For example, due to the limited availability of physical space, Hong Kong's resort is much smaller than its Californian counterpart, while Tokyo's park is bigger for the opposite reason. As mentioned in chapter 2, these four cities – Tokyo, Paris, Hong Kong, Shanghai – have occupied top positions within global city rankings, starting with Tokyo which was identified by Saskia Sassen in her foundational study as a leading global city along with New York and London, reflecting the then dominant geographical triad within world capitalism: East Asia, Western Europe and North America (Sassen, 1991).

In the following twenty-five years, despite the shift towards a more multipolar world in economic terms (the newly founded G20 forum started representing this emergent plurality from the late 2000s onwards), these macro-regions have retained their economic hegemony, as shown by the continued importance of the G8 summits, grouping a select number of powerful countries, all from the West, apart from Japan, as Russia was excluded in 2014 after the geopolitical tensions in Ukraine. At the same time, East Asia has seen a shift in economic leadership from Japan to China. In the 1980s, Japan came to be seen as the only country rivalling the USA's economic and technological primacy. However, this rapidly proved to be an illusion, as by the late 1980s the overheated Japanese economy had crashed, with prolonged stagnation in subsequent years. In contrast, from the 1990s onwards China has undergone a steady process of economic ascendancy, culminating in 2010 when it reached the second position in terms of GDP after the USA, overtaking Japan. As a result, today's Japanese economy is highly dependent on exports to China as regards both consumption and capital goods.

Over the years, Disney's localization strategy has reflected this changing configuration of the world economy, particularly in East Asia. When Disney established its presence in the early 1980s, Tokyo was amidst a process of urban and economic restructuring. This was characterized by flexible production at the firm level (the Toyota lean production system replaced Fordist mass production as the dominant pattern of industrial organization) and by socio-economic transformations typical of global cities, such as the expansion of producer services and the financial sector, as well as the increased internationalization of its economic structure (Fujita, 2003). Within the public sphere, this process was reflected in the urban branding policy pursued by the metropolitan government in the name of 'Tokyo Renaissance' and 'Tokyo Frontier' (Machimura, 1992), inspired by similar campaigns conducted at that time in Western cities, most notably the famous 'I love New York' campaign (see Greenberg, 2008).

The opening in 1992 of a Disney park in Marne la Vallée, a *ville nouvelle* located in the Île-de-France, the urban region surrounding Paris, is another foundational moment for at least three reasons. First, Euro Disney began its operations only two months after the Treaty on European Union was signed in Maastricht, thus showing the growing appetite for Europe as an area of economic and symbolic investment among multinationals like Disney, as the name originally given to the amusement park testifies, but more generally as a space of renewed well-being and coexistence in the post-Cold War era. At the peak of this pioneering stage in the 'European project', US economist Jeremy Rifkin authored a book significantly entitled *European Dream: How Europe's Vision of the Future is Quietly Eclipsing the American Dream* (Rifkin, 2004). Only a few years later, however, the crisis of the Eurozone originally sparked by the financial crash of 2008 – and the consequent re-emergence of the North–South divide across the continent – quickly shattered these expectations. Second, in the early 1990s the Île-de-France was an example of post-Fordist, highly diversified economy, bringing together the high-fashion sector of the city of Paris (particularly flourishing in the central area known as the *sentier*, in the 2nd *arrondissement*, historically specializing in textile manufacturing) with the high-technology industries scattered across the outer urban region (Storper, 1993). Third, Euro Disney was created on the basis of a partnership between the French government and Walt Disney Company, which led to the building of a new urban complex called 'Val d'Europe'. This settlement was governed through a dedicated regional planning authority, which was intended to support American investors. In this sense, Euro Disney is an example of straightforward adoption of a distinctively North American form of supposedly postmodern urbanism, the Edge City (Garreau, 1991), understood as a fictitious, consumption-led re-creation of an urban environment in suburban areas, usually in proximity to major transport infrastructures such as airports and motorways (Bontje and Burdack, 2005).

With the start of the new millennium Disney has eventually landed in the most powerful emerging economy in the globalized world, China, opening resorts in Hong Kong in 2005 (which had returned to mainland China in 1997 as a Special Administrative Region, after decades as a British protectorate) and in Shanghai in 2016. As with previous locations, the identification of these two cities is also highly illustrative of Disney's constant monitoring of the changing configurations of the world's economy. Indeed, over the last two decades, although Beijing has retained its political and cultural centrality, while Shenzhen and other cities in the Guangdong province have become the hotbeds of China's manufacturing miracle, these two cities have been customarily associated with China's ascent in the global economy. Hong Kong has become a paradigmatic example of urban entrepreneurialism within scholarship on global cities, illustrating the way in which the imperative of global urbanization has replaced that of firm internationalization in contemporary elite discourse (Jessop and Sum, 2000). On the other hand, Shanghai's re-globalization strategy (Wu, 2003) has been at the centre of the so-called Open Door Policy pursued by the Chinese government since 1978, which culminated in 1993 with the creation of the Pudong New Area, a Special Economic Zone that has become home to a globally renowned financial and trade zone, not only for economic reasons but also for its concentration of iconic high-rise buildings such as the Oriental Pearl Tower and the Shanghai World Financial Centre. The adoption of Shanghai as an economic model for globalizing cities in the emerging South, such as Mumbai, characterized by state-sponsored foreign investment, has become a recurrent and even obsessive motif within global discourse. As such, it overshadows the role played by less visible regions and cities, relying on endogenous entrepreneurship, whose contribution to China's economic ascendancy has been even more decisive according to analysts contesting the conventional view of Chinese capitalism (Huang, 2008). The association of Hong Kong with Shanghai to form China's 'windows on the world', to borrow Ulf Hannerz's definition of urban cosmopolitanism as a process of transnational connection (Hannerz, 1996), is not new, as it traces its origins back to the colonial period, when the two cities were used by the British Empire as international trade outposts with China. However, this association has been strongly reinforced by the advent of globalization: as Ackbar Abbas puts it, 'Shanghai and Hong Kong have always had a special relation to each other, if only through their relationship to the rest of the world' (Abbas, 2000: 773). This process of global urbanization has not been without losers as well as winners: in 2010, the year in which Shanghai was immersed in the celebrations for the world's Expo entitled Better City Better Life, in which Western corporations such as Siemens and IBM showcased their investment in technology-intensive urban infrastructure, international mass media reported widespread demolitions entailing the eviction of long-term residents to make way for the new Disneyland site (Richburg, 2010).

While Disney's trajectory brings to the surface the Western colonial unconscious that is commonly hidden behind the official rhetoric of globalization and cosmopolitanism, the next and final section of this chapter will deal with a softer manifestation of cultural homogenization whose colonizing effect is no less pervasive in the contemporary urban experience.

GUGGENHEIMIZATION: RE-CREATING THE MAGICAL AURA OF THE CAPITALIST CITY

Writing in 1936, the great German intellectual and independent scholar Walter Benjamin famously theorized the way in which the technological reproducibility of artwork in contemporary capitalism – particularly illustrated by the film industry – replaced the unique sense of magical aura originally associated with art, given by the sensory experience of the distance between the viewer and the work of art:

> In even the most perfect reproduction, one thing is lacking: the here and now of the work of art – its unique existence in a particular place. It is this unique existence – and nothing else – that bears the mark of the history to which the work has been subject. This history includes changes to the physical structure of the work over time, together with any changes in ownership. (Benjamin, 2006: 103)

Although this short essay soon became a masterpiece of critical theory, at the time of its publication Benjamin's idea of lost aura, as well as his confidence in the possibility of creating alternative oppositional movements within the emerging mass culture (Kellner, 2005), drew critiques of romanticism and idealism. These included complaints by an eminent member of the Frankfurt School, Theodor Adorno, regarding Benjamin's lack of engagement with a dialectical understanding of the role of culture and art in capitalist societies, oscillating between myth and reconciliation (Adorno, 1980). It is in this context of growing dissatisfaction with the sense of loss of authenticity in contemporary artwork, particularly when attached to the experience of contemporary life, that one can look at the re-creation of a mythical dimension for art fruition and representation through the reinvention of uniqueness in the architectural form of venues for modern art, such as museums and other exhibition spaces from the 1930s onwards. The attempt at re-creating art's magical aura was particularly epitomized by the project of a new building dedicated to the Solomon Guggenheim Museum in New York, a project that was famously assigned to Frank Lloyd Wright, a major representative of modernist architecture in the USA. Since its founding as an informal exhibition space in the 1930s, the Solomon Guggenheim collection was devoted to the so-called non-objective painting: abstract art was both a response to the reification of artwork and a reflection of the increasingly pervasive process of real abstraction in capitalist societies, as was theorized by Lukács, Benjamin, Adorno and the other Frankfurt School thinkers at that time (see Jameson, 1979).

The subsequent Guggenheim Museum project took a long time to be accomplished, exactly sixteen years, being conceived in 1943 and eventually concluded in 1959, a few months after Lloyd Wright's death. The project is commonly associated with the charismatic figures of Frank Lloyd Wright and Solomon Guggenheim, but an important – though long-unacknowledged (Dunlap, 1987) – role was played by Robert Moses, the powerful and highly controversial city planner who dominated New York's scene for about four decades, from the early 1920s to the early 1960s (Caro, 1975). Despite the fact that he was not a fan of Lloyd Wright's experimental architectural style, having preferred a more conventional design for the new Guggenheim Museum, he nevertheless played a decisive role in pushing the museum project forward, by exerting pressure on city officials over the approval of the planning permit for the new building after years of bureaucratic impasse. The site of the museum was identified along Fifth Avenue, in the wealthy Upper East Side and just in front of Central Park, whose renovation in the 1930s had been undertaken under his aegis. In his recount of the modernist refashioning of New York in the twentieth century and the key role played by Robert Moses in the process, Marshall Berman has distinguished between the first phase before the Second World War, in which Moses promoted visionary projects such as Jones Beach and several parks and gardens including Central Park, and the second phase, in which Moses aligned his name with controversial, car-centred urban renewal projects such as the Bronx Expressway and the failed Lower Manhattan Expressway (Berman, 1982). The latter, especially, made history, as it sparked opposition from local residents, particularly in Greenwich Village, in which Jane Jacobs – the great urbanist – took part, being inspired by this activist experience in the writing of her seminal critique of modernist urban renewal (Jacobs, 1961).

Jacobs' plea for the preservation of thriving neighbourhoods and a socially dense urban fabric was bound to prevail with the general public over Moses' modernist understanding of urban planning from the 1960s onwards, leading to his political decline. As Marshall Berman points out, Robert Moses' trajectory was illustrative of the wider New Deal policy course in the USA and the related conception of state-driven capitalist modernization, of its potentials as well as its pitfalls and contradictions. The Guggenheim Museum, therefore, has to be understood against the background of this hegemonic project of capitalist modernization, in which New York occupied a central role in economic, political and cultural terms. Ironically, this modernist, state-led project of urban and societal government started unravelling soon after the completion of the museum. In this context, the museum with its powerfully seductive architectural form was intended, on the one hand, to reinstate a sense of magical aura in the experience of art fruition; on the other hand, it was intended to revitalize a sense of iconic consciousness and emotional belonging to an urban environment whose authenticity had been undermined by the impersonal aesthetic of the post-war modernist and concrete-laden projects of urban renewal.

This function of the Guggenheim project can be better understood by drawing on Bob Jessop's reformulation of the Gramscian notion of hegemonic bloc in a context of urban regime and governance analysis:

> hegemonic projects [...] help secure the relative unity of diverse social forces. A hegemonic project achieves this by resolving the abstract problem of conflicts between particular interests and the general interest. This project mobilizes support behind a concrete program of action that asserts a contingent general interest in the pursuit of objectives that implicitly or explicitly advance the long-term interests of the hegemonic class (fraction) and thereby privileges particular corporate-economic interests compatible with this program while derogating the pursuit of other particular interests that are inconsistent with the project. (Jessop, 1997: 62)

Although generally overlooked in scholarly accounts of Moses' era, the New York Guggenheim Museum project is illustrative of the project of capitalist modernization pursued by Robert Moses and the related hegemonic bloc during the post-war years, in the context of what is known now as 'spatial Keynesianism' (Brenner, 2004), in which national, regional and local authorities support urban redevelopment processes through budget deficit policies, particularly financing public works. The attainment of the museum project itself was instrumental in the building of a cultural hegemony around the larger process of urban redevelopment being pursued by the city government under the guidance of Robert Moses, whose interventions raised controversies and conflicts.

Along related lines, we can interpret the creation of new Guggenheim museums over the last three decades, particularly in Bilbao and those under way in Abu Dhabi and Helsinki (in Abu Dhabi it is expected to open in 2017, while in Helsinki the process is still nebulous, as mentioned in chapter 1). The Bilbao Guggenheim Museum opened in 1997 following an initiative by the regional government, which offered to the Guggenheim Foundation the funding necessary for the construction of the new museum. The project has sparked lively debates about the so-called 'Guggenheim effect' on urban development, particularly in terms of tourism attraction but also of imposition of a strictly consumption-oriented pattern of culture-led regeneration (Gómez and González, 2001). When the proposal was put forward, in the early 1980s, the city of Bilbao was coping with a process of deindustrialization deeply affecting its manufacturing base. In the subsequent years, Bilbao saw a process of entrepreneurialization of city governance, with a public–private partnership taking the lead in urban regeneration initiatives. In this context, the Guggenheim Museum, planned in the derelict port area, whose design was assigned to the Canadian architectural star Frank Gehry, became the flagship initiative of the urban regeneration strategy. According to Sara González, the museum is at the core of the project of discursive rescaling and repositioning within the global arena being pursued by local politico-economic elites in search of a novel 'spatio-temporal fix' after the decline of its Fordist economy (González, 2006). From the point of view of local elites, the project has achieved its goals, not only in terms of attraction of international tourists in a city where tourism was previously almost non-existent, but from a broader perspective in terms of construction of a 'model city' being propagated on the global level through a process of policy dissemination (González, 2011; see chapter 2).

The Guggenheim project in Abu Dhabi, the political capital of the United Arab Emirates, has been the second major step in the process of globalization of the Guggenheim. Minor exhibition spaces have been opened also in Venice and Berlin, and, while the latter is no longer operating, both have had a relatively low impact on their urban environments in symbolic and economic terms, compared with the spectacular projects of New York and Bilbao and with those in the making in Abu Dhabi and Helsinki (in Venice the Guggenheim Museum is located in a pre-existing historical building). Originally planned in 2006 and also assigned to Frank Gehry, the execution of the Guggenheim in Abu Dhabi has been repeatedly postponed due to the advent of the financial crisis in the late 2000s (in 2009 the Abu Dhabi government had to bail out the suffering Dubai World investment company). However, at this stage, the Guggenheim Abu Dhabi already exemplifies the pursuit of cultural hegemony as a combination of consent and coercion, as this notion was originally conceived by Antonio Gramsci (Lears, 1985). As part of the Saadiyat cultural island project (a concentrated reproduction of Western cultural icons, such as the Louvre, the Royal Albert Hall and the Guggenheim itself), the Guggenheim project reflects local elites' willingness to reconcile capitalism, mass culture and the preservation of the orthodox Islamic mores as a way of consolidating their power (Ponzini, 2011). In doing so, on the one hand, the Guggenheim project reproduces the regime of severe labour exploitation behind the recent wave of spectacular urban development in the United Arab Emirates, despite the vibrant protests led by organizations advocating the rights of the migrant workforce of mainly Indian and Pakistani descent (Chen, 2016). On the other hand, the museum also aims to accomplish its cultural mission through an ambitious 'centre for contemporary Arab, Islamic, and Middle Eastern culture'. This hegemonic project is therefore justified on the grounds of the pursuit of an ideal of art as a 'unique existence in a particular place', as conceptualized by Benjamin in his famous critique of the mechanical reproducibility of artwork. As a reproduction of two seemingly homogeneous but inevitably differentiated entities (as expressions of different politico-economic contexts and related hegemonic blocs), such as the 'original' Guggenheim in New York and the subsequent Bilbao Guggenheim, the Abu Dhabi Guggenheim embodies Deleuze's idea of singularity as the 'repetition of difference' (Deleuze,

1994). Jennifer Robinson has shown how the principle of juxtaposition of repetition, difference and the production of singularities is at the heart of the contemporary phenomenon of cities becoming increasingly globalized entities through relational processes (Robinson, 2016; see also chapter 2). The spatio-temporal succession of Guggenheim museums is a powerful demonstration of this dynamic: an overlapping and intricate juxtaposition of different urban stories and corresponding politico-economic projects of hegemony, rather than a straightforward replication of an original model.

Helsinki is the latest destination in Guggenheim's global flight. The decision to create a Guggenheim museum in the capital of Finland was originally taken in 2011, on the basis of an agreement between the Guggenheim Foundation and the city of Helsinki. After some vicissitudes (the first plan was put aside in response to criticism raised by the artistic community and the wider public), in 2015 the city of Helsinki announced the results of the architecture competition for the design of the new building. The partnership between the city of Helsinki and the Guggenheim Foundation produced an ambitious feasibility plan, analysing in detail the economic return of the investment in which the state of Finland was called to contribute in a substantial way (The Solomon Guggenheim Foundation, 2011). The analysis was set against the backdrop of Helsinki's and Finland's economic and cultural conditions, whose general outlook was considered positive at that time, as the Finnish economy ranked second in the European Union – the report underlined – in terms of global competitiveness according to the World Economic Forum. Despite the economic downturn caused by the 2008 financial collapse, which led to a sudden contraction of Finland's GDP in 2009 (8.3 per cent less than the previous year), in line with the other Baltic countries, Finland's economy was still apparently healthy in 2011, as it had promptly recovered from the Great Contraction (in 2010 the GDP had grown again, by 3 per cent). However, the recovery soon proved to be an illusion, as since 2011 the country has entered a recession which is still affecting its economy, while other EU economies have resumed at least tepid growth paths. In previous years, Finland's economic fortunes and, particularly, the rise of Helsinki as a 'technopole' playing a leading role in the ITC sector on a global scale (Pelkonen, 2005) had been closely associated with the worldwide dominance of Nokia products. However, since the late 2000s Nokia mobile phones have been declining in popularity due to the ascent of the new generation of smartphones. The resulting irreversible decline of Nokia and the ITC sector in Finland became evident in 2013 when Nokia sold its mobile devices business to Microsoft (Viita, 2014). The loss of Nokia has been traumatic for Finland, not just in terms of conventional signs of economic restructuring (job losses and decreasing exports), but perhaps more importantly in terms of national identity and 'corrosion of character', to paraphrase Richard Sennett's (1998) essay. In that essay, the noted sociologist analysed the sense of personal disorientation originating from the decline of big bureaucracies and organizations, including large corporations, and the advent of an era of flexible work and contingent affiliations within post-Fordist societies (Sennett, 1998). At the time of writing, however, the materialization of the museum is still uncertain, due to the lack of general agreement on the project. In a way, Guggenheim's invitation by Helsinki's political elites can be seen as an attempt at filling the void left by Nokia in a context of economic shrinkage. However, the difficulties surrounding the project reveal how this idea was illusory and, in many respects, dictated by the traumatic loss of Nokia. For its part, Helsinki's urban community looks at a re-energized urban environment as the way forward in the pursuit of a renewed prosperity. A high-tech scene is taking shape in Helsinki around an emerging start-up community (Bosworth, 2012), particularly thanks to the role played by newly created, business-oriented institutions such as the Aalto University, which merges three pre-existing universities specializing in technology, business and economics, and art and design. Put simply, what can be learnt from the Helsinki experience is that the Guggenheim could not take the place of Nokia as a pivotal actor forging the nation's identity: it is the city itself that is in a position to replace Nokia at a time in which the innovative capacity of capitalism is no longer confined within the walls of a firm but stretches across society as a whole, with cities – as condensations of 'general intellect' in today's knowledge-intensive capitalism – being particularly fertile grounds for the entrepreneurialization of society, as the following chapter explores in greater detail.

CONCLUSION

This chapter has critically reappraised the phenomenon of societal homogenization brought on by the advent of globalization. When globalization took hold as an increasingly hegemonic discourse within contemporary societies in the early 1990s, social scientists engaging with a critical analysis of the postmodern condition particularly looked at this phenomenon, coining notions such as McDonaldization, Disneyfication and Guggenheimization, to make sense of this process of socio-cultural colonization of the world based on the diffusion of Western lifestyles and mass culture.

Re-examining that literature, this chapter has reached the following four conclusions: first, as theorized by Frederic Jameson, the postmodern condition shows continuity with the twentieth century and, as argued here, it can be considered a 'spatio-temporal moratorium' of late capitalism, as conceptualized by the founders of critical thinking in continental Europe. On the other hand, however, the deepening of globalization – understood as a constitutively intricate rather than linear process of cumulative expansion at the planetary level – entails the fact that the adoption of these Western icons in other world regions takes the form and meaning of a 'repetition of difference', as Jennifer Robinson puts it, rather than a straightforward reproduction of an allegedly original model, as these appropriations are always embedded within specific political-economic pathways and related hegemonic forces and governance structures. Third, in one way or another, these forces have played a foundational role in the penetration of the culture of global capitalism in the respective contexts: from the McDonaldization of food culture and wider social behaviour in the post-socialist societies of China and Russia, to the Disney parks in Orlando and in Paris, which are prominent examples of the adoption of a neoliberal logic of urban governance, and the Guggenheim project in Abu Dhabi, illustrative of the uses and contradictions of urban development in that context. Fourth, in line with the crisis of the mega-event briefly analysed in chapter 1 with reference to the troubled Olympic Games in Rio de Janeiro in 2016, the prolonged impasse of the Guggenheim project in Helsinki reveals a crisis of the mega-project as a catalyst for city entrepreneurialism and an engine of urban economic growth. In the final instance, this raises questions about an increasingly impending move towards the city at large as a site of economic valorization predicated on the entrepreneurialization of society and the self in contemporary capitalist societies, which will be analysed in the following chapter.

5 | Variations ————————————————

CITIES IN AND AFTER THE GLOBAL ECONOMIC CRISIS: THE PRESENT AS HISTORY

The 'civilizing process' analysed in the previous chapter is illustrative of a distinctive feature of the contemporary age of global capitalism: the adoption of consumption patterns and related modes of economic, societal and spatial organization in disparate cities across the world, especially those located within regions that have embarked on a process of capitalist transformation of their economies and societies. This 'civilizing process' has fostered belief in Western and particularly American capitalism, which has spread across the globe since the end of the Cold War era. At the same time, as already anticipated, despite the persistence of Western forms of cultural domination based on hegemonic actors like those analysed in the previous chapter, the neoliberal governmentality of contemporary capitalist societies pushes towards an economic valorization of the social fabric of cities as a whole. This chapter is concerned with the ambivalence of this process of valorization. In order to understand this process, a preliminary clarification of the use of the related notions of 'variegation' and 'variation' is necessary.

The proponents of the notion of 'variegation' (Brenner et al., 2010) have aimed to go beyond the institutionalist assertion of variety among national political economies, based on the geographical variation of prevailingly firm-centred institutional mechanisms and regulatory regimes in different domains: from market coordination to corporate governance, from financial intermediation to labour markets (Amable, 2003; Hall and Soskice, 2001). This nation-centred understanding of the diversity of capitalism and the systems of economic regulation has not been a prerogative of the so-called varieties-of-capitalism approach. Michel Foucault, in the lectures collected in *The Birth of Biopolitics*, in which he provided his path-breaking definition of neoliberalism, also built his reflection on the recognition of national variants such as 'American neoliberalism', the 'German neo-liberal model' and the 'French project of social market economy' (Foucault, 2008).

What Foucault could not take into account at the time of his writing was the advent of globalization and its consequences on social life. In an accurate critical review of the scholarship dealing with the varieties of capitalism, Jamie Peck and Nik Theodore underlined the problems related to the adoption of methodological nationalism (the fact that nation-states remain uncontested units of analysis), particularly the normative assumptions underlying comparative exercises (Peck and Theodore, 2007). The article called for the embrace of a critical economic-geographical approach to the study of 'variegated capitalism', although the authors did not explore in depth the ways in which variegation can be used as an operational concept. Useful insights in this respect are provided by Bob Jessop, who has started elaborating an alternative framework for the analysis of variegated capitalism, suggesting the use of notions of compossibility, complementarity, competition, rivalry and antagonism among different modes of capital accumulation within a global context characterized by the ecological dominance of neoliberalism, in contrast to the static typologies of the mainstream varieties-of-capitalism literature (Jessop, 2011).

A substantial advancement in our understanding of variegation is also provided by Peck and Theodore in a journal article co-authored with Neil Brenner, in which they have come to theorize the variegation of neoliberal modes of societal government against the backdrop of the global economic crisis: 'a systemic production of geoinstitutional differentiation' triggered by the intensification of neoliberalization processes across the world (Brenner et al., 2010). This definition particularly illuminates the way in which variegation actually works in contemporary societies characterized by the heightened mobility of policy imperatives of 'good governance', 'global competitiveness' and 'austerity' in times of crisis. From this perspective, variegation has to be understood against the backdrop of neoliberal governmentality, acting as a 'global logic' constantly circulating across the world and being adapted to different economic-political and cultural-institutional settings. However, while usefully combined with the policy mobility perspective (see chapter 2), this approach is too reliant on geography as an ultimately decisive factor in variegation processes, thus replacing economy with geography as a determinant 'in the last instance' of social processes, to put it with – *mutatis mutandis* – Althusser's classic redefinition of the structure-superstructure relationship. In the final analysis, from this perspective neoliberalism appears as an external force rather than as a constitutive element of global capitalism. The purpose of this chapter is precisely to explore the immanence of neoliberal governmentality to contemporary capitalism.

Elaborating on a previous article which theorized varying forms of capitalism at the urban and regional scales beyond the mainstream of institutionalist and political economy approaches (Rossi, 2013a), the idea of 'variations' in the city–capitalism nexus is intended to highlight the differentiated (both negative and affirmative) ways in which the neoliberal project of entrepreneurialization of society and the self is pursued within a context of knowledge-intensive and life-oriented global capitalism. In doing so, a combined usage is offered of Bob Jessop's concept of 'societalization' and Giorgio Agamben's and Paolo Virno's materialistic ontology of forms-of-life. This is in order to call attention to the ambivalent ways in which contemporary capitalism engages with processes of societalization and production of forms of life within advanced liberal societies. In particular, the aim of this chapter is to show how contemporary cities reflect and at the same time actively contribute to neoliberal capitalism's imperative of entrepreneurialization of society and the self. The shift to an increasingly deeper entrepreneurialization of society and the self is not understood as a linear process of succession in which subsequent stages of economic development follow each other, but rather as an intricate, constitutively ambivalent, stratification of modes of societalization and forms of life, reflecting the mutating macroeconomic conditions of contemporary capitalism, constantly oscillating between austerity- and growth-driven strategies of governance.

The remainder of this chapter is dedicated to illustrating how the combination of a strategic-relational political economy approach and a materialistic ontology helps us explain the variations of today's city–capitalism nexus, thus challenging common interpretations of geography and nationally bounded institutional systems as determinants 'in the last instance' of capitalist variegation.

Societalization

The starting point here in the theorization of city–capitalism variations is the fact that capitalism has acquired a global form, where the notion of 'the global' is understood in a twofold sense: as a geographical term, underlying the idea that globalization has enabled capitalism to expand across the globe; and as a defining characteristic of contemporary capitalism, deriving from its tendency to commodify an increasing number of spheres of social life, as this book has emphasized in different parts. In doing so, however, it is important to avoid conveying an essentializing, metaphysical understanding of capitalism as an impersonal force somehow naturally or mechanically expanding across space and society with diversification effects. Rather, capitalism's geographical and societal extension and its changing configurations have to be viewed as the outcome of historically situated politico-economic projects of societalization in a global context of neoliberal dominance. These projects rely on 'social structures of accumulation', broadly defined by the proponents of this concept as 'all the institutions that impinge upon the accumulation process' (Gordon et al., 1994: 14). In contemporary critical urban theory, this idea demands attention being paid to the mobilization of actors, coalitions, discursive formations and related governmentalities in the pursuit of constantly changing capital accumulation strategies. In this context, a key reference is the work of Bob Jessop, particularly his strategic-relational rereading of capitalism through Marxist lenses (see also chapter 4).

Jessop's approach builds on the idea of societalization as a departure point for an analysis aimed at identifying the social structures of accumulation and related strategies being pursued by hegemonic coalitions (reflecting a 'historical bloc', in classic Gramscian terminology). This concept has taken shape within the framework of Bob Jessop's original attempt to 'put state theory into place' (Jessop, 1990):

> the existence of society cannot be taken for granted: it must be constituted and reproduced through more or less precarious social processes and practices which articulate diverse social relations to produce a 'society effect'. (Jessop, 1990: 5)

This definition calls into question the role of the state, which has been central to Jessop's intellectual project, and the ways in which societalization projects brought about by what Jessop called 'accumulation strategies, state strategies and bourgeois hegemonic projects' take form (Ibid: 7). Along these lines, for instance, Jessop understood Thatcherism in Britain as a project of corporatist societalization aimed at a 'radical realignment' of social forces, which ultimately gave rise to an irreversible rupture with the post-war social-democratic compromise. In his subsequent book on the future of the capitalist state, Jessop more explicitly touched on the issue of variation, arguing that:

there is wide variation in how far capitalist market forces (and the associated logic of profit-seeking) come to dominate the overall organization and dynamics of social formations [...]. This raises questions about the conditions under which accumulation can become the dominant principle of societal organization (or societalization). (Jessop, 2002b: 16)

In this book, he provided an overview of the shift from 'Atlantic Fordism' and Keynesianism to post-Fordism and the Schumpeterian competition state, the latter being founded upon the incessant pursuit of technological innovation and a knowledge-based economy characterized by the 'ecological dominance' of neoliberal capitalism. The notion of 'ecological dominance' is important here, as it offers a starting point for an analysis of 'global capitalism' and its urban manifestation. At this stage of his intellectual path, Jessop was already aware of the fact that 'interest in varieties of capitalism' and their respective strengths and weaknesses coincides with 'increasing recognition of mutual complementarities and rivalries' and 'possible evolutionary and adaptive benefits in maintaining institutional diversity' (Ibid: 102); an understanding of variation which he elaborated further in the coming years. However, throughout this book he persistently referred to national and macro-national varieties of capitalism, associated with the key players of the globalized capitalist economy, such as the USA, Japan, the European Union and, increasingly, China (see Jessop, 2002b: 102).

In what follows, the intent is to challenge the 'methodological nationalism' informing varieties-of-capitalism research, despite being aware of the main limitations of conventional critique of methodological nationalism (see Beck and Sznaider, 2006), notably its quick dismissal of the state as a relevant unit of analysis within social science research and the rather naive (and uncritical) embrace of cosmopolitanism as an allegedly impartial outlook on capitalist societies

(Calhoun, 2002; Chernilo, 2006). In doing so, this chapter aims to replace both geographical variegation and nation-centred institutionalism as outcomes of different political economy strands (and also of Foucault's political thought, as said above), with an emphasis on the global reach of the neoliberal entrepreneurialization of society and the self as a constitutive component of contemporary knowledge-intensive capitalism.

In order to do this, this chapter will first engage with a materialistic-ontological redefinition of capitalism, one which is attentive to the production of fluctuating forms of life and the ambivalent use of life itself in a context of knowledge-intensive capitalism. This exercise will enable us to get rid of the methodological essentialism (expressed in its nation-centred form) of the mainstream varieties-of-capitalism approach, as well as of the limitations of the variegated neoliberalization thesis, eventually designating a set of different regimes of societalization illustrating the ambivalence of global capitalism.

Forms of life

In his recent book *The Use of Bodies*, presented by the author as the final stage of an intellectual path he commenced with the publication of *Homo Sacer* two decades earlier (Agamben, 1998), Giorgio Agamben has offered a redefinition of ontology based on the notion of 'forms of life', beyond metaphysics (Agamben, 2016). Agamben takes as a departure point of his analysis the centrality acquired by language contra the transcendental within 'non-professional philosophers' (as he calls them), such as Nietzsche, Benjamin and Foucault, and within contemporary societies, where language commonly overlaps with the human being. Against this background, he comes to terms with modern ontology, by engaging in 'an archaeology of ontology'. His reflection starts from the unsolved split between ontology and logic, between being and existence, between potential and act, a dilemmatic divide that traces its origins back to Aristotle (Agamben, 2016). To solve the puzzlement of ontology, Agamben resorts to the notion of 'demand', which he associates with Spinoza's concept of *conatus*. In his view, this notion allows us to break the fixity of the human being imposed by ontological apparatuses (for the notion of apparatus, see also Agamben, 2009; on its relationship to the varied forms of capital accumulation and regulation, see Rossi, 2013a). The demanding being is one that constantly 'modifies, desires, and constitutes itself' (Agamben, 2016: 171), giving rise to an ever-growing number of modes of being. In this sense, he conceptualizes the mode of being as a rhythm, which is by definition mobile and fluid, thus refusing a schematic crystallization of essence: the being is a flow and the substance modulates itself within the modes, Agamben concludes. The being, therefore, does not appropriate the modes of being; rather, it defines itself through the modes themselves. This 'modal ontology' is instrumental in Agamben's theorization of 'use' – his main objective in this book – as an alternative to act as a realization of the human being. Use cannot be considered a mere activity, nor a possession of something; rather, it is a form-of-life arising from a reiterated engagement with what defines one's life. The example of the pianist clarifies this idea:

> Glenn Gould, to whom we attribute the habit of playing the piano, does nothing but make use-of himself insofar as he plays and knows habitually how to play the piano. He is not the owner or the holder of the power to play, which he can or cannot enact, but he constitutes himself as someone making use of the piano, irrespective of the fact of playing or not playing it. Use, as a habit, is a form-of-life, rather than knowledge and the individual ability to do something. (Agamben, 2016: 61–2)

In conclusion, in Agamben's view the being cannot be separated from habit and use and, therefore, from a form-of-life. The emphasis placed by Agamben on the notion of 'use' can be clarified by looking at an essay in which Paolo Virno puts forward the notion of 'usage of life'. In particular, he argues that the usage of life is presupposed on a process of distantiation from the self, comparable with that of the actor willing to perform different roles within an endless training process (Virno, 2015). The usage of life consists of this multiplicity of roles. According to Virno, this versatility potentially breaks with the individualistic care of the self identified by Michel Foucault and other neo-Foucauldian theorists, preparing the ground for the rise of a sense of 'us', which makes possible the enactment of forms of life that are alternative to the neoliberal logic of individualization.

Along these lines, the remainder of this chapter identify three moments reflecting a 'modulation' of the being – to put it in Agamben's terms – with respect to the neoliberal regularity of the 'entrepreneur of the self' originally identified by Foucault: formation, crisis and reassertion. The formative stage is associated with the transitional condition of the 'socialized city', which exemplifies the subsumption of society into the mechanisms of capital valorization. The subsequent section will then focus on the 'dispossessed city', a condition that is illustrative at one and the same time of the organic crisis affecting global capitalism and its relentless continuation of forms of life originally associated with 'primitive accumulation' under conditions of structural crisis and fiscal austerity. Finally, the chapter will identify a 'revenant city', as an illustration of the process of capitalist re-embeddedness and ever deeper re-socialization. The alternation of these stages should not be conceived in a linear fashion, but as an intricate process of stratification. In crisis-ridden capitalist economies, characterized by what some economists term the 'secular stagnation' (see the introduction), the 'dispossessed city' is not merely a temporary state of emergency but becomes a permanent condition, overlapping with the development of affirmative biopolitical economies in the context of what is called 'here the revenant city'. It is in this context that the multiple roles theorized by Paolo Virno in his idea of the 'usage of life' become more evident.

Societalization processes and the varying modulations of the forms of life in contemporary capitalism are analysed with particular (but not exclusive) reference to the USA and the European Union. The former is the country where the first global, systemic crisis of the globalization era originated, and it is also the economy that has more quickly left behind the Great Recession and the subsequent economic impasse in the world economy while reproducing its distorted economic development model based on financialization: it is currently viewed by its own most authoritative news media outlets simultaneously as an 'island of stability' (Irwin, 2016) and as a concentration of 'economic illness' (Foroohar, 2016). The European Union, on the other hand, is where one can more clearly observe the societal effects of the regime of fiscal consolidation in a context of persistently anaemic growth, acting as a role model for austerity-driven governance, but also being mobilized by alternative forces as a space for a potential politics of emancipation, particularly at the city level. This contradictory role played by the USA and the European Union takes place within an increasingly turbulent global economy, where the European Union is struggling with a persistently anaemic growth, the new economic powers of Brazil, Russia, China and South Africa (the so-called 'BRICS') are grappling with growing economic uncertainties, and emerging markets like Indonesia, Turkey and Nigeria, amongst those that in previous years witnessed an unprecedented economic expansion, are contravening previous expectations of fast growth or have already been affected by major economic downturns.

THE SOCIALIZED CITY

Nature builds no machines, no locomotives, railways, electric telegraphs, self-acting mules etc. These are products of human industry; natural material transformed into organs of the human will over nature, or of human participation in nature. They are *organs of the human brain, created by the human hand*; the power of knowledge, objectified. The development of fixed capital indicates to what degree general social knowledge has become a *direct force of production*, and to what degree, hence, the conditions of the process of social life itself have come under the control of the general intellect and been transformed in accordance with it. To what degree the powers of social production have been produced, not only in the form of knowledge, but also as immediate organs of social practice, of the real life process. (Marx, 1973: 706)

In this now famous passage which appeared in the 'Fragment on Machines' in the *Grundrisse*, Marx foresaw the advent of a technology-intensive capitalism, in which general social knowledge becomes, in his words, the 'direct force of production'. In this text, in order to make sense of the process of incorporating social knowledge in the capitalist process of valorization, Marx coined a notion that he never used again, general intellect, a term echoing Rousseau's concept of *volonté géné-rale* and perhaps even more directly Aristotle's idea of 'active intellect' (Virno, 2007). This short piece has been at the centre of a lively strand of thinking known as Italian post-*operaismo* (or post-workerism), the continuation of a pre-existing intellectual and political radical move-ment which originally appeared in the early 1960s, asserting the causal relationship between class antagonism and capitalist transformation: class struggles precede and prefigure the restructuring of capitalism, while the consequent reconfigurations of capital open up new space for workers' power. Along these lines, and in a way somehow remi-niscent of Edward Thompson's innovative history 'from below' of the English Industrial Revolution (Thompson, 1963), in the 1990s Paolo Virno interpreted the post-Fordist transition as a 'counter-revolution', a capitalist incorporation of workers' insurgent social behaviours in the late 1960s and the 1970s, centred on the refusal of standardized work and the discipline associated with Fordism's factory organization (Virno, 1996a). Similarly, rehearsing the argument originally made by management consultant Peter Drucker, who famously contended in the 1970s that in the USA the working and middle classes 'collectively own the means of production' through their pension and mutual funds (Drucker, 1993: 60), economist Christian Marazzi has interpreted the financialization of the capitalist economy as a conservative response – i.e., a draining of savings from household economies to stocks and securities – to the 'communism of capital' ingrained in investment schemes that are typical of the 'new economy' (Marazzi, 2012).

Within this scholarship, the publication of Antonio Negri's *Marx Beyond Marx: Lessons on the Grundrisse* in 1979 can be considered the starting point for a new phase of (post-)workerist thinking, which after a somnolent decade in the 1980s (when many of its proponents were imprisoned or forced into exile) underwent a revival in the 1990s and the first decade of the 2000s. In this book, Negri emphasized how Marx envisaged a steady increase in productivity led by technological advances, which indicated how 'we must pass from the extraction of absolute surplus value to the organization of relative surplus value, from the formal subsumption to the real subsumption of society by capital' (Negri, 1989: 131). Marx's notion of general intellect has been at the centre of lively debates in the 1990s. In particular, authors from different disciplinary backgrounds, such as Paolo Virno (a philosopher) and Christian Marazzi (an economist), have suggested going beyond a mere identification of the general intellect with machines and other tangible forms of fixed capital, calling attention to the centrality of language within the post-Fordist economy: not just the elite of highly skilled professionals or, more colloquially, 'smart people' who are identified as knowledge and creativity workers by mainstream economists (Florida, 2012; Moretti, 2012), but the generality of the workforce employed in a variety of economic sectors, from the service economy such as health and social care, entertainment and retail, to the manufacturing industry reproducing the Toyota model of collaborative lean production. In different ways, all members of the workforce are required to adopt a positive disposition towards communicative-relational action in the workplace, as these authors argue (see, for instance, Marazzi, 2011). In this sense, as Paolo Virno points out, a definition like 'immaterial labour', which includes low-income 'cognitive workers' (a term used by other post-workerist authors such as Antonio Negri and Maurizio Lazzarato) or the more elitist 'creative class' (Richard Florida's famous label), is untenable, as such definitions entail that only specific portions of the workforce make an intensive use of knowledge and creativity. It is, rather, the entire 'socialized' workforce that has become 'loquacious' and potentially inventive.

> I have never used the expression 'immaterial labor'; to me it seems equivocal and theoretically inconsistent. Post-Fordism certainly cannot be reduced to a set of particular professional figures characterized by intellectual refinement or 'creative' gifts. It is obvious that workers in the media, researchers, engineers, ecological operators, and so on, are and will be only a minority. By 'post-Fordism', I mean instead a set of characteristics that are related to the entire contemporary workforce, including fruit pickers and the poorest of immigrants. (Virno in Joseph, 2005: 29)

In the Western world, alongside the incipient financialization processes, the 1970s and the 1980s saw the rise of concomitant phenomena of deindustrialization, rising crime rates in the major cities and the individualization of the employment relationship. In this context, feelings of 'opportunism, fear and disenchantment' became predominant (Virno, 1996b). Local politico-economic elites accommodated and deepened this societal reconfiguration of capitalism, labour and related forms of life in post-Fordist times. In particular two articulations of this 'societalization' project can be identified: first, a spatial line of intervention characterized by the embrace of place-based initiatives of urban regeneration aimed, on the one hand, at preventing any manifestation of crime and social deviance through aggressive police tactics (epitomized by the zero tolerance campaign embraced by Mayor Giuliani in New York in the 1990s and continued by Mayor Bloomberg in the following decade) and, on the other hand, by exploiting the consumption and entertainment potential of contemporary cities, involving a wide array of urban settings, such as waterfronts, historic centres, ex-industrial areas and, most notably, neo-bohemian neighbourhoods; second, a societal line of intervention aimed at re-creating the social bases of the contemporary capitalist city after the dissolution of the Fordist-Keynesian social compact, through the mobilization of discursive formations celebrating the virtues of creativity, conviviality and hospitality, in order to attract professional talents and consumers.

The mobilization of these virtues does not entail their generation through, for instance, financial support for public educational institutions, which are on the contrary increasingly underfunded, particularly in socially deprived urban areas. Recently, for example, the Chicago State University – whose campus is located in a disadvantaged area of the south side of Chicago, drawing the vast majority of its students from African-American and Hispanic minorities – has declared 'financial exigency' due to 'state budget mess' (Cohen and Garcia, 2016).

An entrepreneurial approach to creativity, conviviality and hospitality is the new orthodoxy defining today's urban condition among policymakers and city managers dealing with the knowledge-based and consumption-led nature of urban economies. This approach to contemporary urbanism cannot be questioned by public policy, which has to prioritize marketing campaigns, partnership building and pro-business urban regeneration initiatives. In this context, ideas of conviviality and hospitality are used in a purely instrumental fashion. For instance, European cities customarily struggle over the attraction of international tourists and other visitors contributing to their economies, but their sense of hospitality vanishes when it comes to welcoming refugees and undocumented migrants, particularly those with religious affiliations such as Islam, in contrast to alleged Western values of freedom and modernity (Massad, 2015).

The rise of the creative and cultural city has resulted, therefore, from the combined outcomes of these two lines of action. Ideas of creative urbanism were already circulating in the 1980s and the 1990s, but they were focusing on the regeneration of the physical environment of mostly deindustrializing cities in a context of 'urban crisis' (Landry and Bianchini, 1995). In the early 2000s, Richard Florida's theorization of the creative class provided urban politico-economic elites with a powerful toolkit to deal with the linguistic and communicative turn of post-Fordist capitalism. In this context, city governments started mobilizing a wide set of spatial governance tools (marketing strategies, hallmark events, urban regeneration projects), along with empirical evidence derived from statistical indexes provided by their advisors (urban development agencies, cultural foundations, consultants): governing cities became an art within societies of advanced liberalism. Far from being a fixed repertoire of institutions and organizations and related contractual relations, urban governance is therefore used as an operational base turning city dwellers into actors who behave responsibly in the public sphere, reorienting their agency towards an idea of socialized urbanism. In this sense, the 'creative class' has to be understood as a hegemonic project and an active societal construction. Creative class policies, in their essence, imply a process of assemblage: a macro-actor – the creative class – is created from scratch by placing some actors in relation to others, even though these actors are not previously related to each other or may have mutually conflicting interests (Ponzini and Rossi, 2010). The invention of this artificial class has entailed an expropriation of language power from the majority of the workforce in the 'socialized city'. As Agamben pointed out:

> whereas in the old regime the estrangement of the communicative essence of human beings was substantiated as a presupposition that had

the function of common ground (nation, language, religion, etc.), in the contemporary state it is precisely this same communicativity, this same generic essence (language), that is constituted as an autonomous sphere to the extent to which it becomes the essential factor of the production cycle. (Agamben, 2000: 114)

The small but resolute demonstrations against Google buses that took place in San Francisco in 2013 (see chapter 3), or the massive uprisings that erupted in the spring of the same year in the main Brazilian cities, led by young people protesting against a rise in mass transit fares and against public money drained by the football world cup while being diverted from health, education and social services, can be understood as 'acts of citizenship' responding to the expropriation of language power in the post-Fordist 'socialized city'. According to Engin Isin, an act of citizenship is a 'rupture in the given' and particularly 'a rupture that enables the actor (that the act creates) to remain at the scene rather than fleeing it' (Isin, 2008: 27). This continued presence at the scene is testified by the fact that these and other protests in cities across the world since 2011 have brought key facts to the fore of public debates. These include the issue of growing inequalities, associated with post-Fordist forms of capitalist urbanization (i.e, creative and high-tech urbanization is systematically accompanied by rising socio-spatial segregation within cities and by widened regional imbalances among cities) and with global capitalism more generally (concentration of income and wealth within a minority of the population). The unexpected success in the US market and globally of Thomas Piketty's *Capital in the Twenty-First Century* (2014), a book that shows how wealth distribution inequalities have constantly deepened during the twentieth century, apart from the post-war decades that saw the rise of the Keynesian social state (the 'Keynesian exception', as the intro-duction to this book put it), is proof of sweeping changes in public opinion. It has taken almost two decades for these critical voices to gain recognition within the public debate. The recession of the global economy following the financial crisis of 2008 has played a key role by bringing to light the contradictions of capitalism, although it has also fostered authoritarian impulses and free-market revanchism in Europe, the USA and, indirectly, in emerging economies like India, as well as increasingly in South American countries since the unravelling of the 'progressive dream' of the 2000s.

In order to understand the current condition of capitalism, particularly seen through the lens of its urban manifestation, and its characteristic ambivalence, special attention is dedicated here to the global economic crisis (commonly known as the Great Recession), arguing that this event created a suspension of capitalism's productive subsumption of society, imposing a variation in capitalist societalization that has taken the form of a normalized 'state of exception' in which dispossession has become the norm of social relations within austerity-led urban regimes.

THE DISPOSSESSED CITY

In his book dedicated to the critical examination of what he calls the 'new imperialism', David Harvey (2003) has drawn on Marx's theory of 'primitive accumulation' to provide a theoretically informed and politically situated explanation of the contemporary dynamics of capitalism in times of neoliberal globalization. In Marx's *Capital* (see Harvey, 2010) as well as in other classical Marxist texts, such as Lenin's *The Development of Capitalism in Russia* (2004) and Rosa Luxembourg's *The Accumulation of Capital* (2003), the concept of primitive accumulation is related to the historical ascent of capitalism as a mode of production and social reproduction. In this classical view, 'primitive accumulation' was achieved through the forcible separation of workers from the means of production and the capitalist expropriation of land and common resources, which in turn created a proletariat with nothing to sell but its own labour to survive. These were the distinctive features of the historical pathway that led to the 'invention of capitalism' between the eighteenth and the nineteenth centuries in the pioneering countries of the Industrial Revolution (Perelman, 2000). As industrialization spread geographically, primitive capital accumulation started relying heavily on state subsidies and government orders, as Luxembourg (2003) originally pointed out with reference to late nineteenth-century Russia.

The concept of primitive accumulation has thus been customarily associated with the historical rise of capitalism, and with its geographical expansion to hitherto non-capitalist environments such as the colonial lands at the time of Marx (for instance, through the enslavement and so-called 'trade' of African people to the colonial plantations). Marx himself was apparently hesitant to recognize primitive capital accumulation as a constantly evolving phenomenon that went beyond the specific spatio-temporalities conventionally identified with the early stages of the accumulation process and the expansion of capitalist social relations in non-capitalist regions (Perelman, 2000). Harvey's theoretical endeavour, therefore, has been to throw light on the continuing relevance of this concept, using it to uncover the contemporary dynamics of neoliberal capitalism. His work marks a turning point in the ways in which critical geographers and other social scientists have understood the notion of primitive accumulation. In his analysis of neoliberal capitalism, Harvey contends that capitalism's process of expansion in times of globalization revives long-standing dynamics of primitive accumulation, including those originally described by Marx:

> the commodification and privatization of land and the forceful expulsion of peasant populations; the conversion of various forms of property rights (common, collective, state, etc.) into exclusive private property rights; the suppression of rights to the commons; the commodification of labour power and the suppression of alternative (indigenous) forms

of production and consumption; colonial, neo-colonial, and imperial processes of appropriation of assets (including natural resources); the monetization of exchange and taxation, particularly of land; the slave trade and usury, the national debt, and ultimately the credit system as radical means of primitive accumulation. (Harvey, 2003: 145)

Over the last thirty years, with the advent of neoliberalism these dynamics appear to have taken place simultaneously in the global North and the global South, making the contemporary world increasingly globalized in newly integrated ways (Glassman, 2006). This process includes the displacement of peasant populations in emerging capitalist countries, such as India and Mexico, and the strengthening of intellectual property rights as well as the privatization of public services (housing, telecommunications, education) in the Western capitalist countries (Harvey, 2003).

The term 'accumulation by dispossession' originally referred to practices of land encroachment in rural and semi-urbanized regions, but its use has been extended to urban dynamics of capitalist development and socio-spatial restructuring. Processes of gentrification and inflating ground rents in urban environments have been interpreted along Marxist lines, drawing on Harvey's rethinking of Marx's theory of primitive accumulation in a context of entrepreneurialized governance and on his more general theorization of capitalist restructuring of the built environment, driven by alternating cycles of over-accumulation and devalorization (López-Morales, 2010). Even without explicit reference to Marxist theories of primitive accumulation, the term 'dispossession' is inherently associated with the displacement of long-term and low-income residents in capitalist cities as a consequence of eviction ordinances or invisible market mechanisms. Given the lexical relation between dispossession and repossession (or 'foreclosure'), the notion of 'accumulation by dispossession' has become intimately associated with the recent global economic crisis, due to its origins and continued reverberations in subprime mortgage markets of financialized capitalism (Strauss, 2009). In the eyes of critical urban scholars, the specific features of the recent economic crisis confirm the validity of Harvey's long-standing interpretation of the capitalism-urbanization strategic nexus based on finance (the second circuit of capital) as a contra-cyclical regulator of economic development (Hernandez, 2009; Buckley, 2012). In this context, 'dispossession' is seen as the capitalist response (the displacement of insolvent residents ordered by banks and property owners) to the crisis generated by the contradictory and self-destructive effects of financialized capitalism and the related phenomenon of 'financialization of home' (Aalbers, 2008).

In the USA, being constantly evicted and forced to move from the place of living was an ordinary way of life for the most disadvantaged fractions of society long before the 2007–9 crisis, particularly for poor families who rented in black inner-city neighbourhoods (Desmond, 2012). The housing and financial crises of the late 2000s, however, led to an explosion of dispossession-through-repossession in the USA and the other countries affected by the bursting of the real-estate bubble, such as Ireland and Spain. Evictions have become so common in the worst-hit economies like Spain that in 2015 the city of Barcelona – still a popular tourist city, since successfully taking advantage of the opportunity of the Olympics of 1992 – elected a mayor, Ada Colau, who had previously not been involved with party politics but became widely known as the leader of a social movement formed in 2009 (the Platform for People Hit by Mortgages) to protest against the rise in evictions caused by the collapse of the property market, which had worsened due to exploitative mortgage lending rules. Since then, Barcelona has become a role model for anti-austerity grassroots political movements embracing the idea of 'rebel cities' (see Harvey, 2012), particularly in economically struggling southern Europe (Naples, in Italy, is another example of successful coalition between local government and radical social movements).

In the USA, accumulation by dispossession in the form of home foreclosure, but also of increased educational exclusion (see the case of the Chicago State University mentioned above) and segregation, has particularly involved minorities historically affected by racial discrimination, such as African-Americans, especially those residing in cities hard hit by the housing and employment crises of the Great Recession (Brewer, 2012; see also chapter 3). A new civil rights movement, mobilizing under the banner of the 'Black Lives Matter' slogan, has gained ground across the country since 2013, after repeated episodes of police violence, particularly the killings of unarmed black people in Sanford in Florida, in Ferguson in Missouri, and in the African-American enclaves of Staten Island in New York City (Day, 2015). All these episodes have occurred in places located within urban conurbations that were hard hit by the housing crisis and related social and ethnic tensions, such as the metropolitan region surrounding Orlando in Central Florida, the northern part of the Greater St Louis metropolitan area, as well as racially segregated neighbourhoods in New York City. At the same time, with a recovery of the housing market, affluent cities have witnessed soaring house prices that increasingly force African-American residents to move to more affordable (and less attractive) urban areas. This forced exodus has been resisted by African-American activists in cities like San Francisco, where the origins of ethnic minority expulsion can be traced back to the urban renewal programmes of the early 1960s (Finamore, 2016). Both the civil rights movement and the 'right to stay put' mobilizations are responses to the constitutively double valence of dispossession. Being deprived of place, human rights or education ('becoming dispossessed') can lead the dispossessed to cope by engaging in movements of resistance and solidarity in their search for a sustaining environment (Butler and Athanasiou, 2013).

The renewed marginalization of African-American communities is only the tip of the iceberg in a phenomenon involving a wider set of low-income groups within a context of austerity urbanism characterized by the exacerbation of the penal wing of the state, the truly distinctive feature of neoliberal regimes according to Loïc Wacquant (Wacquant, 2012). The new wave of austerity measures brought on by the Great Recession in Europe (most intensely in southern Europe but also in northern countries such as Britain, Ireland and Finland), as well as in the USA (where several dozen municipalities, counties, utility authorities and other special districts like county-owned hospitals and school districts have filed for bankruptcy since 2008, in different states across the country, from California to Michigan), can be interpreted as the extension of the logic of dispossession as a form of life characterizing especially vulnerable groups to the governance of cities as a whole. As Jamie Peck points out, far from being a mere déjà vu of the austerity policies of the 1970s and 1980s, the more recent round of austerity urbanism has taken hold within already neoliberalized societies, being transformed by previous rounds of governmental downsizing and financialization of urban development (Peck, 2012).

At the same time, as argued by Maurizio Lazzarato, the age of austerity has coincided with the return of sovereignty and new forms of 'big government', through a centralization and multiplication of government intervention in the society: not only the intensification of punitive measures brought to light by the 'Black Lives Matter' movement in the USA, but also in the European Union the adoption of increasingly more pervasive procedures of audit evaluation, expenditure monitoring and the imposition of long-term programmes of fiscal consolidation (Lazzarato, 2012). In this context, the state reasserts its control over citizens' lives through increasingly invasive procedures of accountability and transparency, justified in the name of economic recovery (see *The Economist*, 2011), as well as through the ability to suspend local administrations' governing capacity in the name of economic rationalization. In doing so, the state can decide to devolve key functions at the municipal level to unaccountable market actors, sometimes pure financial entities, such as the private equity firms that in the USA have increasingly taken over public services like emergency care and firefighting (Ivory et al., 2016).

Dispossession therefore becomes the organizing principle regulating social and institutional relations at a time of 'late neoliberalism': a stage of neoliberalism deeply permeated by the durable effects of the global economic crisis on government–citizens' relationships. It is in this context that the city has become witness to a 'double movement' of dispossession and resistance by the dispossessed, a phenomenon that has deeply shaped local politics but is reflected also in the ambivalent forms of collaborative economies proliferating within post-recession cities, as discussed in the next section.

THE REVENANT CITY

The last decade has seen a confrontation between austerity- and growth-driven politics taking place within contemporary cities: on the one hand, urban environments have been severely hit by the financial crash of 2008, in terms of both socio-spatial restructuring (job losses, economic shrinkage and stagnant housing markets) and the effects of the austerity measures adopted by local governments in response to policies of fiscal retrenchment dictated by national and supranational institutions (especially in the European Union), as well as the financial stress affecting over-indebted municipal budgets; on the other hand, over the same time period, cities and metropolitan areas have acquired a renewed role as economic-cultural engines of capitalism, in two closely interrelated ways – the formation of high-technology clusters formed by start-up businesses particularly concentrated in the inner-city districts, and the phenomenon of the technology-based 'sharing economy'.

As discussed throughout this book, both these phenomena have spread rapidly across numerous cities in the world, thus becoming a truly global experience. The point of departure here is the phenomenon of high-tech start-ups proliferating in urban areas across the world. Different sources identify the emergence of leading 'start-up cities' in a variety of geographical contexts: from South America (such as Santiago de Chile, Rio de Janeiro and São Paulo) to Europe (London, Berlin and Paris), Asia (Tel Aviv, Istanbul, Dubai, Singapore and Shenzhen) and also Africa (Lagos and Cape Town). In many respects, the original model city was Tel Aviv, therefore outside the USA, where the local technology institute in the neighbouring town of Haifa – the Technion – has stimulated an unprecedented growth of technology-oriented entrepreneurship. However, in recent years, leading high-tech cities in the USA, such as New York, San Francisco and Boston, have been at the centre of what *The Economist* has called 'The Cambrian moment':

> Start-ups are a big part of a new movement back to the city. Young people increasingly turn away from suburbia and move to hip urban districts, which become breeding grounds for new firms. Even Silicon Valley's centre of gravity is no longer along Highway 101 but in San Francisco south of Market Street. (*The Economist*, 2014: 2)

Urban start-up economies are illustrative of a process of re-enlivenment of capitalist economies within urban social environments. The urban high-tech entrepreneur is simultaneously embedded within localized communities and economic 'ecosystems' and defines herself through a global sense of belonging fostered by social media and transnational networks, unlike first-generation post-Fordist entrepreneurs who limited their allegiance essentially to the local and regional scales.

Generally speaking, as capitalist economies are constitutively unstable economic systems, major economic crises and the consequent evolutionary pathways are key to processes of re-embeddedness and dis-embeddedness. In many contemporary cities, the advent of the start-up phenomenon in technologically innovative sectors entailed the decline and even the marginalization of previously 'innovative' firms in ICT and other technology sectors which had appeared during the previous stages of post-Fordist transition towards an 'information society'. In Turin, Italy, for instance, a post-industrial city where the local institute of technology has been at the forefront of university-led processes of business incubation, politico-economic elites emphasize the need to modernize technology-oriented sectors and to open the doors to a new generation of high-tech firms, more flexible and globally oriented than the traditional ICT sector (Rossi, 2016).

Far from being a natural process of global expansion, the start-up phenomenon is actively supported by geographically ramified think thanks, foundations and professional networks, the majority of them based in the USA, which are committed to activities of dissemination and sensitization, exerting strong influence over the public sphere. In 2012, Startup Weekend, a no-profit organization based in Seattle and supported by the Kaufmann Foundation (a key proponent and disseminator of the global discourse around start-up economies and cities), was reported to have helped organize more than 2,000 events in more than 100 countries.

While the so-called Siliconization projects of the 1980s and the 1990s (technopoles, science parks, ICT districts) were mainly policy-led experiments pursued by the entrepreneurial state in a late-Keynesian fashion (Castells and Hall, 1994), in the new booming high-tech economies the community dimension is dominant at the symbolic level. For instance, in New York – commonly regarded as an example of a 'model high-tech city' – the local meet-up group (allegedly the largest in the world with its 40,000 members) organizes major meetings on a monthly basis, while minor events are available in the city on a daily basis, being organized by other communities of technologists and institutions variously involved in the high-tech scene.

This community dimension represents the competitive advantage of successful high-tech economies, which have benefited from the technological and broader societal changes brought on by the advent of the communication channels offered by the so-called Web 2.0 (such as social media and online professional networks). Using an analytical framework originally put forward by Jodi Dean (2009), it can be argued that this phenomenon is illustrative of an age of 'communicative capitalism' nourished by a set of animating fantasies such as 'abundance' (there is never enough information and innovation), 'participation' (everyone can launch an entrepreneurial venture) and 'wholeness' (anyone can be part of *the* community, of *the* high-tech scene in New York or elsewhere), but one might also add cooperation and community itself. The sense of excitement about belonging to a community that characterizes start-up entrepreneurs is central to the revitalization of capitalism as a 'happiness industry' (Davies, 2015; see also Ahmed, 2010) after the suffering connected with the economic crisis and the age of austerity. Cities, where technology-based forms of life have flourished in recent years, are required to play a central role in this fabrication of happiness (Florida et al., 2013). Being a tech entrepreneur, therefore, entails adopting an 'integral form-of-life', based on a characteristic combination of emotions, habits and modes of relationality, rather than simply embarking on an entrepreneurial project. The term 'integral form-of-life' is intended to bring together Gramsci (via Jessop) and Agamben: through the notion of *economia integrale* (integral economy), as Bob Jessop has pointed out, Gramsci meant the structural coupling of an economic base and the related forms of social regulation (Jessop, 1990). Similarly, the notion of integral form-of-life entails the overlapping of forms of life and governmental rationalities within post-recession neoliberal societies.

It would be misleading, however, to think of urban high-tech districts as purely self-organized entities, an idea conveyed by the official representation of this phenomenon. The ideal of self-organization is another pillar of the culture of capitalism in the digital era (Uitermark, 2015). Along with foundations and different types of consultancy agencies, local and national governments also play an important role, especially in cities aspiring to become magnets for venture capitalists and other investors supporting high-tech business formation. Rather than assuming an explicitly directional role, as in the (late) Keynesian era of technopoles, city administrations and national governments support these processes by investing in public discourse and promotional strategies (marketing campaigns have been particularly pervasive in the promotion of the 'Tech City' in London), but also in human capital through a special emphasis placed on training programmes and the creation of high-profile institutions specializing in high-tech education (such as the Cornell Tech campus project launched by Mayor Bloomberg in New York), the entrepreneurialization of society being the goal of pro-growth urban policy in post-recession neoliberal societies.

The 'revenant city' is, therefore, illustrative of capitalism's use of 'organic crises', such as the recent 'great contraction', as opportunities for re-embedding itself within societal relations, thus reinventing its dominant culture and related forms-of-life. The sharing economy is a manifestation of the advanced subsumption of society and life itself as key to the capitalist process of recovery and reinvention. It is no surprise that the phenomenon of the sharing economy has exploded in the post-recession years. Pioneering companies such as Airbnb and Uber were founded in 2008 and 2009, respectively, but gained popularity after the end of the recession in the USA. Airbnb expanded its operations by over 126 per cent in 2011 (Wauters, 2012), the year in which economic indicators of GDP growth clearly show that the US economy started to grow again after the recession. This dynamic is illustrative of an advanced process of subsumption involving life itself. While the start-up phenomenon involves a potentially unlimited multitude of professional (sometimes only aspiring) entrepreneurs and illustrates the shift from the entrepreneurialization of society to that of the self, the sharing economy testifies to the materialization of Michel Foucault's idea of entrepreneurialization of the self (Gordon, 1991), as everyone is now expected to make a profit from possessions in an entrepreneurial way.

This process of entrepreneurialization of the self attempts the reconciliation of two mutually excluding social processes: individualization and community. On the one hand, the sharing economy mobilizes a distinctively urban sense of openness to the other: the home-sharing economy, for instance, is based on the idea of making domestic space accessible to strangers, turning the encounter with the stranger into an exciting rather than fearful experience. This touches on what Iris Marion Young, drawing inspiration from Roland Barthes, defined as the eroticism of city life: 'the pleasure and excitement of being drawn out of one's secure routine to encounter the novel, strange, and surprising' (Young, 1990: 249), making the sharing economy a highly attractive opportunity. However, the erotic experience of the encounter with the stranger, Young adds, is 'the obverse of community' as 'in the ideal of community people feel affirmed because those with whom they share experiences, perceptions, and goals recognize and are recognized by them; one sees oneself reflected in the others' (Ibid: 250). To address this contradiction and the relative sense of disorientation, the corporate proponents of the sharing economy obsessively lay emphasis on the supply of a web-based community. However, the experience of community ends up being a mere narcissistic exhibition of the self in the Internet space offered by the hosting company. Despite the illusory attempt at creating a 'community' (an 'animating fantasy' in Jodi Dean's words), the process of 'individualization', as Foucault would put it, is the distinguishing feature of the official sharing economy. Foucault indeed defined 'the government of individualization' as 'everything which separates the individual, breaks his links with others, splits up community life, forces the individual back on himself, and ties him to his own identity in a constraining way' (Foucault, 1982: 781).

In response to this process of individualization, a wide range of cooperative economy initiatives has formed, experimenting with a different 'use of life', which is intended to revive a 'sense of us' in contrast to the individualizing, highly commodified, sharing economy. In cities in Europe but also in the USA, self-managed initiatives of cooperation have taken form at the grassroots level in a context of austerity and have then stabilized, such as citizens' networks, co-housing projects, solidarity purchase groups and other experiments of community management and co-ownership. Within the web, activist groups have given rise to different forms of alternative collaborative economies. In a recent essay, Trebor Scholz has identified a number of examples of what he calls 'platform cooperativism', understood in opposition to the 'platform capitalism' of the official sharing economy and the larger web 2.0 (Srnicek, 2016), including the so-called 'city-owned platform cooperatives' which he defines as 'a city-designed software/enterprise, similar to Airbnb that could serve as online marketplace owned and democratically controlled by the people who rent space to travelers' (Scholz, 2016: 16). Outside the web, within actually existing urban spaces, recent years have seen an equally resurgent interest in cooperative housing projects where city dwellers 'weave new networks of trust and care amid the alienating pressures of the capitalist cityscape' (Huron, 2015: 977). These social projects call into question what Elizabeth Povinelli terms 'the problem of ethical substance in late liberalism', namely 'the question of the endurance, let alone the survival, of alternative forms of life in the gale force of curtailing social winds' (Povinelli, 2011: 14), or what authors like Giorgio Agamben (see earlier in this chapter), Antonio Negri and Frédéric Lordon, who have drawn on Spinoza's concept of *conatus*, would define 'the perseverance in being' in either a transformative or a preservational sense for the existing capitalist order (Negri, 1991; Lordon, 2014).

Alternative projects, therefore, show that one should not think of processes of social and life subsumption within contemporary capitalism in a mono-directional and totalizing way. According to an increasing number of authors, within and outside academia, alternatives to the official, corporate-led sharing economy provided by the voluntaristic efforts of activist movements and citizens' groups are illustrative of the opportunities for social transformation offered by contemporary capitalism. These authors speculate over the deeper implications behind the proliferation of post-capitalist experiments of 'commoning' within contemporary societies, founded on reciprocity rather than on market-led mechanisms of property-based exchange, arguing that there is a potential of post-capitalism within actually existing capitalist societies (Mason, 2015). Some authors in this strand place emphasis on the centrality of technology for a revitalized progressive agenda, looking at the ways in which today's post-capitalist social movements embrace the technological challenge, rather than refusing it a priori, as was the case in traditional radical groups (Srnicek and Williams, 2015). Writing from a more mainstream perspective, influenced by Elinor Ostrom's institutionalist theorization of the commons, Jeremy Rifkin – a popular business guru who has acted as adviser to important Western governments and the European Union – has argued that elements of reciprocity and gratuity are at the heart of contemporary digital technologies, as the collaborative commons phenomenon in the web 2.0 paradigmatically shows (Rifkin, 2014). While in the early 1990s Peter Drucker provocatively identified a post-capitalist potential in the socialized ownership structures of financial capitalism, authors who emphasize the emancipatory potential of contemporary technologies contend that post-capitalism is immanent in the forms of life, not just the forms of social interaction but more deeply in the fluctuating forms of life, understood as the different ways that people make use of their lives and the multiple roles they perform within technology-based everyday economies.

Technology companies, however, are smelling opportunity in the idea of communal life. Since 2015, for-profit co-living spaces have been set up in trendy neighbourhoods such as Williamsburg and Crown Heights in Brooklyn, New York City, but also in less established areas like Spring Garden in Philadelphia and North Acton in London (Kaysen, 2015; Kasperkevic, 2016). One of these companies explicitly appropriates the notion of the commons in its brand, reproducing at the same time the communication style of a champion of the home-sharing economy like Airbnb, while another one has started a co-living business called 'The Collective' in a high-rise building, promising to offer a 'new lifestyle for Londoners'.

CONCLUSION

The interpretation offered here of the variations of capitalism as seen in its urban manifestation differentiates from previous theorizations of the varieties of capitalism but also of variegated neoliberalization in three ways. First, even though it builds on the assumption of the hegemony of neoliberalism, it refuses an institutionalist-geographical determination of the variations of capitalism, an approach still predominant in contemporary urban and regional scholarship, which looks at variation as either the manifestation of ideal-type patterns of economic and societal governance associated with specific nation-states, regional spaces or macro-regions, or as the outcome of processes of geographical circulation of ideas, policy recipes and expert knowledge.

Second, it looks at neoliberalism as a governmental rationality closely intertwined with the constitution of knowledge-intensive capitalism, particularly of its socialized and biopolitical economies and related phenomena of entrepreneurialization of society and the self, rather than as a somewhat external force circulating across the globe on the initiative of politico-economic elites, as in the variegated-neoliberalization approach and related strands of research such as the scholarship investigating the role of policy mobility in shaping global urbanization (see chapter 2).

Third, it offers a 'presentist' view of today's capitalist societies (the idea of the 'present as history' presented in the introductory chapter of this book), understood as intrinsically indeterminate formations reflecting the rapidly mutating macroeconomic conditions of the global economy and the political alternatives arising from them. In doing so, the approach proposed here escapes any historicist temptation that still inhabits contemporary Marxist theory, including its post-dialectical formulations, but also institutionalist assumptions of path-dependency. In the final analysis, the evolution of global capitalism is understood as an intricate process of stratification, rather than a linear trajectory, leading to a condition of ambivalence whose political implications will be discussed further in the conclusion of this book.

Conclusion: _____
Living in the Age of Ambivalence

This book has dealt with the relationship between cities and capitalism at a time of advanced globalization and late neoliberalism. The context in which this relationship currently takes form is deeply influenced by the financial crisis of 2008 and its aftermath, particularly what is commonly known as the 'Great Contraction' of the global economy. At the time of writing, eight years after the event of the crisis, the world economy is still far from having attained rates of GDP growth comparable to those that were considered normal before the global economic crisis. Even though conditions of stagnant low growth seem to be limited to the European Union, there is a perception that even the more stable US economy has structural weaknesses, mostly related to the illness of financialization, which could sooner or later lead to another major crisis. At the same time, the economic slowdown in many emerging markets, along with global threats such as climate change, the new wave of anti-Western terrorism and a number of unresolved geo-political tensions, exacerbates fears related to this anaemic growth and the perceived instability of global capitalism. This situation particularly affects the middle class in both the affluent countries of the West and the developing economies, giving rise to new forms of economic populism but also to protests led by a 'no-future' youth generation and racial minorities already afflicted by precarious working conditions, difficult access to housing, meagre salaries and growing indebtedness.

Against this backdrop, it has become commonplace to point out that the current economic scenario gives rise to ambivalent developments at the political level. On the one hand, there is a wave of 'chauvinistic populism', particularly illustrated in the USA by Donald Trump's triumphant nomination as a presidential candidate of the Republican Party, but also by related phenomena of post-political citizen-led parties (such as the Five Stars Movement in Italy) and the new wave of Islamophobia in Europe, by the authoritarian drift in India and by the successful anti-EU ('Brexit') campaign in the United Kingdom led by the former mayor of London, Boris Johnson, and the UK Independence Party. On the other hand, a renewed transformational politics has gained wide currency since 2011, especially in response to the growing inequalities characterizing contemporary capitalist societies, as brought to light by a variety of 'deep-democratic' movements across the globe (Purcell, 2013), from the radical Occupy Wall Street Movement to the more liberal-oriented umbrella movement in Hong Kong and the recent *Nuit Debout* protests in Paris.

These political and social phenomena can be seen as two sides of the same coin: the former can be considered a (deformed) copy of the latter. They are radically opposed to each other, but at the same time one is the mirror image of the other. The mainstream media point to the populist character of both, namely to the fact that both the new conservatives inspired by the Tea Party in the USA and the new progressive leaders inspired by the post-2011 social movements (Bernie Sanders in the USA, Jeremy Corbyn in the UK, Pablo Iglesias in Spain, Alexis Tsipras and Yanis Varoufakis in Greece) have imported into the political arena claims made at the grassroots level. However, a more substantive interpretation of this ambivalence can be offered, one grounded in the analysis of contemporary capitalism. In 1993, only a year before Berlusconi entered the scene of Italian politics that he occupied for more than twenty-five years, *Luogo Comune*, a short-lived, non-academic journal of political theory, in which Paolo Virno and Giorgio Agamben were active, amongst others, published an unsigned collective editorial titled 'Theses on New European Fascism' which put forward the following argument: contemporary fascism is the 'twin brother', or the 'disturbing double', of a transformational conception of politics that has come out of the crisis of representative democracy in previous decades. As such, it can no longer be viewed as a state-centred political-ideological project, as it was in the 1920s and the 1930s, but instead must be seen as a pathological response to the erosion of modern sovereignty brought on by the advent of post-Fordist economies, with their emphasis on the dismantling of labour relations and the socialization of production through the use of communication and language as productive forces (Luogo Comune, 1993). In making this argument, *Luogo Comune* was not referring to the far right movements, and was not even referring to Berlusconi (as he was still outside politics, even though his political ascent began only one year later), but was referring to the wider anti-political stance informing the transition from the First to the Second Republic in Italy in the early 1990s.

The similarities with what is happening today are striking. Many commentators have noted how Donald Trump seems to be a repetition of Berlusconi, and even the mainstream media now warn about the risk of fascism in the USA (Douthat, 2015; Kagan, 2016), although their analyses draw a veil over the socio-economic foundations on which new forms of fascism rely. Cities and their societal configuration in post-Fordist and neoliberal times are an essential part of these foundations. This is immediately discernible at a surface level, comparing Trump to Berlusconi. The latter started his business trajectory in the construction sector, being mainly associated with the 'private city' project named *Milano Due* (or Milan Two), conceived in the 1970s as a suburban reproduction of the affluent lifestyle characterizing the city of Milan. In subsequent years, he established himself as a mass-media tycoon before entering politics. Similarly, Trump has shifted from the construction sector to mass media, even though his reputation as a business man is more associated with the former than the latter, starting with the iconic Trump Tower in Manhattan, while Berlusconi can be considered a 'political entrepreneur' capitalizing on post-Fordism's communicative turn (Lazzarato, 1994). Both Berlusconi and Trump are illustrative of the urban roots of contemporary post-Fordist capitalism, where the city accounts not only for the investment opportunities in the built environment as a highly financialized sector but also for the cognitive and communicative capital that can be extracted from their societies. But Trump, like Berlusconi, is only the most visible manifestation of the current wave of 'new fascism' that infests politics and the wider society in the West, stimulating a sense of revanchism within the white middle class. As *Luogo Comune* presciently diagnosed: 'postmodern fascism inhabits not the closed rooms of a government office, but the kaleidoscope of metropolitan forms of life' (Luogo Comune, 1993: 6).

In Italy, symptoms of 'metropolitan fascism' became apparent during the latest global economic crisis, when Berlusconi's political trajectory was already declining. In December 2013, amidst the austerity-led process of economic and social restructuring, Italian cities saw an explosion of social discontent led not by the labour unions or the progressive political parties, as in previous economic crises, but by self-organized groups belonging to an impoverished, politically under-represented, middle class comprising small contractors, street vendors, self-employed workers and unemployed youths. The ex-Fordist city of Turin, in previous decades associated with impetuous eruptions of the working class (in July 1962 the unexpected revolt of the Piazza Statuto in Turin anticipated Italy's subsequent wave of working-class uprisings, from 1969 through to the late 1970s), was the stronghold of the protest, witnessing the closure of the vast majority of shops and street markets for two entire days, with no involvement of the official trade unions, while spontaneous protests erupted all across the city. Italy's national flag replaced the red flag customarily exhibited in general strikes, though still in limited number. These events and the emotional situation of frustration and social resentment from which they originated resembled what Karl Polanyi described when he wrote about historical fascism as a spectre constantly looming over capitalist societies coping with the failure of a self-regulating market economy: 'fascism was an ever-given political possibility, an almost instantaneous emotional reaction in every industrial community since the 1930s. One may call it a "move" in preference to a "movement"' (Polanyi, 2001: 247).

The intention of this book has been to provide a closer examination of the forms of life associated with contemporary capitalism that simultaneously revive the spectre of fascism and allow the rise of a transformational politics. In doing so, this text has looked behind this level of visibility, interrogating today's increasingly inextricable city–capitalism nexus as the realm of the ambivalent. Having identified the foundations of this nexus (the long-term 'emergences' of entrepreneurialism, financial power and cognitive capital identified in chapter 1), and having scrutinized its evolving global dimension (chapter 2), as well as its short-term continuities and geographical diffusions across the planet (in chapters 3 and 4), the fifth chapter of this book analysed the way in which the city becomes a primary site where the neoliberal project of the entrepreneurialization of society and the self materializes. The crisis of 2008 has led to an eradication of the residual legacies of universalism inherited from the twentieth century, such as the welfare state and a representative democracy. In the West, which has been particularly hit by the economic crisis, the recent wave of fiscal austerity has intervened in already neoliberalized societies, producing a double sense of dispossession, as described in chapter 5 of this book. In the emerging economies, economic turbulence is shattering illusions about a painless transition from an export-led to a consumption-led economic development model, while the recent commodity crisis has brought to light the vulnerability of oil-dependent countries, fomenting authoritarian impulses in South America and the Middle East, but also of the global economy as a whole, as it is associated with its deflationary tendencies, mirroring earlier concerns about new forms of nationalistic politics spurred by increasing fuel prices and expected shortages of oil (Mitchell, 2011).

As a result of these differentiated dynamics, global capitalist societies are experiencing a new wave of individualization processes, particularly rooted within the dynamics of urban economies. A widespread invocation of community, but also a sense of frustrated expectations arising from ephemeral senses of belonging, takes form as a result of this process of individualization (Joseph, 2002). However, as Michel Foucault first noted, within advanced liberal societies the government of individualization conceals the very existence of community (see chapter 5). The start-up and sharing economy phenomena, but also the commons-oriented cooperative efforts, which have proliferated in post-recession cities are a powerful illustration of how the individualization of economic agency has produced an idealization of community in different ways: from the energizing meet-ups organized by start-up entrepreneurs to the web-based opportunities for socialization offered by the sharing economy, to the grassroots practices of 'commoning'.

In a book collecting articles written between the 1990s and the early 2000s, dedicated to the process of individualization in contemporary 'second modernity', Ulrich Beck and sociologist Elisabeth Beck-Gernsheim recognized the ambivalence of the contemporary social structure, where the experience of 'becoming an individual' can turn into a situation of either isolation or integration and independence (Beck and Beck-Gernsheim, 2002). From their perspective, one should neatly distinguish between two competing understandings of individualization: the neoliberal idea of the free-market individual, which they align with 'Anglo-Saxon societies', and what they call 'the sense of institutionalized individualization'. The former is associated with a utilitarian experience of isolated atomization; the latter reflects the shift towards the reflexive societies of second modernity where 'the individual is not a monad but is self-insufficient and increasingly tied to others, including at the level of worldwide networks and institutions' (Ibid: xxi). The 'sub-politics' and the 'life politics' advocated by Ulrich Beck and Anthony Giddens respectively, both centred on the empowerment of the self-reflexive individual, are predicated on the normative assumption of an enlightened civil society putting private concerns at the centre of public debates in response to the disintegration of collective solidarities produced by the advent of a 'disorganized capitalism' (Giddens, 1991; Beck, 1997).

In Beck as in Giddens, in Habermas and generally in the optimistic views of the social-liberal theorists writing in the 1990s, neoliberalism is judged as a degenerative force that can be averted through the pursuit of dialogue and consensus, allowing rational problem-solving in life-related controversies. For its part, this book has understood neoliberal governmentality as intimately interlinked with contemporary urbanism, which has become a constitutive element of knowledge-intensive capitalism in both negative and affirmative ways: processes of dispossession, displacement and dis-embeddedness have overlapped with those of economic resurgence and the production of a new capitalist subjectivity, drawing on the cognitive capital of cities. The re-production of socio-spatial unevenness is inseparable from the reinvention of urban economic development capitalizing on the 'commonwealth' of urban societies. During the post-recession years, urban economies are being deeply reshaped by the advent of a wide range of experience economies, in which conventional boundaries between production and consumption, between labour time and leisure time, are increasingly blurred. However, existing regulations are persistently favouring profit-driven strategies, shifting risk from corporations to workers formally recruited as independent contractors (in the USA those who offer services in this new economy typically belong to ethno-racial minorities living in major cities and other urban-dwelling disadvantaged groups: Steinmetz, 2016b), thus weakening labour protection and driving down wages

(Asher-Schapiro, 2014). In addition, as discussed throughout this book, the neoliberal rationality restricts to a circumscribed set of actors (variously termed 'the creative class', 'urban techies', 'smart labour') the entitlement to represent the creativity of urban societies, even though the city as a whole is mobilized as a source of social innovation. The common wisdom is reluctant to acknowledge these intertwined contradictions and ambivalences of contemporary capitalism. As a result, the cooperative potential of capitalist societies remains unexpressed or captured within a neoliberal logic of individualization, while the over-exploitation of the middle class channels social frustrations and racist sentiments into the public sphere.

In contemporary neoliberal societies, even the idea of the 'commons' is not exempt from profit-driven valorization or selected access to allegedly 'common goods'. In post-crisis transitional times the commons can be mobilized for mutually excluding purposes (see Enright and Rossi, forthcoming): to reinforce a pro-market logic of individualization, renewing the rent-extraction logic of capitalism, as in the neo-capitalist narrative of the official sharing economy discourse; to produce novel institutions of life in common in response to the disruptive effects of a broken neoliberal economy. Re-politicizing urban life along emancipatory lines is therefore essential for uncovering the ambivalence and the injustices of the global urban condition in a context of neoliberal dominance. As Lauren Berlant puts it: 'the question of the political becomes identical with the reinvention of the infrastructures for managing the unevenness, ambivalence, violence, and ordinary contingency of contemporary existence' (Berlant, 2016: 394).

References

Aalbers, M. (2008) The financialization of home and the mortgage market crisis. *Competition and Change* 12(2): 148–66.

Aalbers, M. (2011) *Place, Exclusion, and Mortgage Markets.* Oxford: Wiley-Blackwell.

Aalbers, M. (2012) (ed.) *Subprime Cities: The Political Economy of Mortgage Markets.* Oxford: Wiley-Blackwell.

Aalbers, M. (Forthcoming) The pre-histories of neoliberal urbanism in the United States. In Morel, C. and Pinson, G. (eds), *Debating the Neoliberal City.* Aldershot: Ashgate.

Aalbers, M. and Christophers, B. (2014) Centring housing in political economy. *Housing, Theory and Society* 31(4): 373–94.

Abbas, A. (2000) Cosmopolitan de-scriptions: Shanghai and Hong Kong. *Public Culture* 12(3): 769–86.

Adorno, T. (1980) Letters to Walter Benjamin. In Bloch, E., Lukács, G., Brecht, B., Benjamin, W. and Adorno, T., *Aesthetics and Politics.* London: Verso, pp. 110–33.

Adorno, T. (2004) *Negative Dialectics.* London: Routledge (1st edn 1966).

Adorno, T. and Horkheimer, M. (2002) *Dialectic of Enlightenment: Philosophical Fragments.* Stanford, CA: Stanford University Press (1st edn 1947).

Agamben, G. (1998) *Homo Sacer: Sovereign Power and Bare Life.* Stanford, CA: Stanford University Press (1st edn 1995).

Agamben, G. (2000) *Means without End: Notes on Politics.* Minneapolis, MN: University of Minnesota Press.

Agamben, G. (2009) *What is an Apparatus? And Other Essays.* Stanford, CA: Stanford University Press.

Agamben, G. (2016) *The Use of Bodies.* Stanford, CA: Stanford University Press (1st edn 2014).

Ahmed, S. (2010) *The Promise of Happiness.* Durham, NC: Duke University Press.

Alonso, W. (1968) Urban and regional imbalances in economic development. *Economic Development and Cultural Change* 17(1): 1–14.

Althusser, L. (2010) *For Marx*. London: Verso (1st edn 1965).

Amable, B. (2003) *The Diversity of Modern Capitalism*. Oxford: Oxford University Press.

Amin, A. and Thrift, N. J. (1995) Institutional issues for the European regions: From markets and plans to socioeconomics and powers of association. *Economy and Society* 24(1): 41–66.

Amos, H. (2014) McDonald's flagship restaurant reopens. *The Moscow Times*, 14 November. Available at: <https://themoscowtimes.com/articles/mcdonalds-flagship-moscow-restaurant-reopens-41542>.

Arrighi, G. (1994), *The Long Twentieth Century: Money, Power, and the Origins of Our Times*. London: Verso.

Arrighi, G. (2004) Spatial and other 'fixes' of historical capitalism. *Journal of World-Systems Research* X(2): 527–39.

Arrighi, G. (2009) The winding paths of capital. Interview by David Harvey. *New Left Review* 56: 61–94.

Aschoff, N. (2015) *The New Prophets of Capital*. London: Verso.

Asher-Schapiro, A. (2014) Against sharing. *Jacobin Magazine Online*, 19 September. Available at: <https://www.jacobinmag.com/2014/09/against-sharing/>.

Audretsch, D. B. and Feldman, M. P. (1996) R&D spillovers and the geography of innovation and production. *The American Economic Review* 86(3): 630–40.

Barber, B. (2013) *If Mayors Ruled the World: Dysfunctional Nations, Rising Cities*. New Haven, CT: Yale University Press.

Barnett, C. (2005) The consolations of 'neoliberalism'. *Geoforum* 36(1): 7–12.

Bartlett, D. (2010) *FashionEast: The Specter that Haunted Socialism*. Cambridge, MA: MIT Press.

Barton, D., Chen, Y. and Jin, A. (2013) Mapping China's middle class. *McKinsey Quarterly*, June. Available at: <http://www.mckinsey.com/industries/retail/our-insights/mapping-chinas-middle-class>.

Basolo, V. (2007) Explaining the support for homeownership policy in US cities: A political economy perspective. *Housing Studies* 22(1): 99–119.

Bauböck, R. (2003) Reinventing urban citizenship. *Citizenship Studies* 7(2): 139–60.

Beaverstock, J., Smith, R. G. and Taylor, P. J. (1999) A roster of world cities. *Cities* 16(6): 445–58.

Beck, U. (1997) *The Reinvention of Politics: Rethinking Modernity in the Global Social Order*. Cambridge: Polity.

Beck, U. and Beck-Gernsheim, E. (2002) *Individualization: Institutionalized Individualism and Its Social and Political Consequences*. Thousand Oaks, CA: Sage.

Beck, U. and Sznaider, N. (2006) Unpacking cosmopolitanism for the social sciences: A research agenda. *British Journal of Sociology* 57(1): 1–23.

Benjamin, W. (2006) The work of art in the age of its technological reproducibility. In Eiland, H. and Jennings, M. W. (eds), *Walter Benjamin. Selected Writings*, vol. 3, 1935–1938. Cambridge, MA: Harvard University Press, pp. 101–33 (1st edn 1936).

Berg, B. F. (2007) *New York City Politics: Governing Gotham*. New Brunswick, NJ: Rutgers University Press.

Berlant, L. (2016) The commons: Infrastructures for troubling times. *Environment and Planning D: Society and Space* 34(3): 393–419.

Berman, M. (1982) *All that is Solid Melts into Air: The Experience of Modernity*. New York: Simon & Schuster.

Blakeley, G. (2010) Governing ourselves: Citizen participation and governance in Barcelona and Manchester. *International Journal of Urban and Regional Research* 34(1): 130–45.

Blitz, R. (2005) Blair's 10-year home ownership goal. *The Financial Times*, 25 January. URL: http://www.ft.com/cms/s/0/0bd6d524-6e76-11d9-a60a-00000e2511c8.html.

Blyth, M. (2012) *Austerity: The History of a Dangerous Idea*. New York: Oxford University Press.

Boltanski, L. and Chiapello, E. (2005) *The New Spirit of Capitalism*. London: Verso (1st edn 1999).

Bontje, M. and Burdack, J. (2005) Edge cities, European-style: Examples from Paris and the Randstad. *Cities* 22(4): 317–30.

Bosworth, M. (2012) Nokia decline sparks Finnish start-up boom. *BBC News*, 13 December. Available at: <http://www.bbc.com/news/technology-20553656>.

Bradsher, K. (2015) India's manufacturing courts the world, but pitfalls remain. *The New York Times*, 14 October. Available at: <http://www.nytimes.com/2015/10/15/business/international/indias-manufacturing-sector-courts-the-world-but-pitfalls-remain.html?_r=0>.

Braudel, F. (1983) *Civilization and Capitalism 15th–18th Century. Volume II. The Wheels of Commerce*. London: Collins (1st edn 1979).

Brenner, N. (1999) Globalisation as reterritorialisation: The re-scaling of urban governance in the European Union. *Urban Studies* 36(3): 431–51.

Brenner, N. (2004) *New State Spaces: Urban Governance and the Rescaling of Statehood*. New York: Oxford University Press.

Brenner, N. and Schmid, C. (2014) The 'urban age' in question. *International Journal of Urban and Regional Research* 38(3): 731–55.

Brenner N. and Schmid, C. (2015) Towards a new epistemology of the urban? *City* 19(2–3): 151–82.

Brenner, N. and Theodore, N. (2002) (eds.) *Spaces of Neoliberalism: Urban Restructuring in North America and Western Europe.* Oxford: Wiley-Blackwell.

Brenner, N., Peck, J. and Theodore, N. (2010) Variegated neoliberalization: Geographies, modalities, pathways. *Global Networks* 10(2): 1–41.

Brewer, R. M. (2012) 21st-century capitalism, austerity, and black economic dispossession. *Souls* 14(3–4): 227–39.

Brown, W. (2015) *Undoing the Demos: Neoliberalism's Stealth Revolution.* New York: Zone Books.

Buckley, M. (2012) From Kerala to Dubai and back again: Construction migrants and the global economic crisis. *Geoforum* 43(2): 250–9.

Bush, G.W. (2004) Acceptance speech to the Republican National Convention. *The Washington Post*, 2 September 2004. Available at: <http://www.washingtonpost.com/wp-dyn/articles/A57466-2004Sep2.html>.

Butler, J. and Athanasiou, A. (2013) *Dispossession: The Performative in the Political.* Cambridge: Polity.

Caldwell, M. L. (2004) Domesticating the French fry: McDonald's and consumerism in Moscow. *Journal of Consumer Culture* 4(1): 5–26.

Calhoun, C. J. (2002) The class consciousness of frequent travelers: Toward a critique of actually existing cosmopolitanism. *South Atlantic Quarterly* 101(4): 869–97.

Camagni, R. (1995) The concept of *innovative milieu* and its relevance for public policies in European lagging regions. *Papers in Regional Science* 74(4): 317–40.

Cameron, D. and Osborne, G. (2015) Here's how to build a home-owning Britain. *The Times*, 4 July. Available at: <http://www.thetimes.co.uk/tto/opinion/article4487691.ece>.

Campbell, T. (2008) Introduction: Bíos, immunity, life: The thought of Roberto Esposito. In Esposito, R. (2008) *Bíos. Biopolitics and Philosophy.* Minneapolis, MN: University of Minnesota Press, pp. vii–xlii.

Caro, R. A. (1975) *The Power Broker: Robert Moses and the Fall of New York.* New York: Vintage Books.

Castells, M. (1977) *The Urban Question: A Marxist Approach.* London: Arnold (1st edn 1972).

Castells, M. (1989) *The Informational City: Information Technology, Economic Restructuring and the Urban-Regional Process.* Oxford: Blackwell.

Castells, M. (1996) *The Rise of the Network Society.* Malden, MA: Blackwell.

Castells, M. and Hall, P. (1994) *Technopoles of the World: The Making of 21st-Century Industrial Complexes*. New York: Routledge.

Celata, F. and Rossi, U. (2009) Industrial districts. In Kitchin, R. and Thrift, N. J. (eds), *International Encyclopedia of Human Geography*. New York: Elsevier, vol. 5, pp. 389–95.

Chaban, M. (2015) Jersey City proposes legislation to legalize Airbnb. *The New York Times*, 11 October. Available at: <http://www.nytimes.com/2015/10/12/nyregion/jersey-city-proposes-legislation-to-legalize-airbnb.html>.

Chen, M. (2016) The Guggenehim doesn't want labor activists interfering with its luxurious Abu Dhabi outpost. *The Nation*, 25 April. Available at: <https://www.thenation.com/article/the-guggenheim-doesnt-want-labor-activists-interfering-with-its-luxurious-abu-dhabi-outpost/>.

Chernilo, D. (2006) Social theory's methodological nationalism: Myth and reality. *European Journal of Social Theory* 9(1): 5–22.

Clinton, B. (1995) Untitled. In *The National Homeownership Strategy: Partners in the American Dream*. Washington, DC: US Department of Housing and Urban Development, unpaged.

Cochrane, A., Peck J. and Tickell, A. (1996) Manchester plays the game: Exploring the local politics of globalization. *Urban Studies* 33(8): 1319–36.

Cohen, J. and Garcia, M. (2016) Chicago State University declares financial crisis due to state budget mess. *Chicago Tribune*, 4 February. Available at: <http://www.chicagotribune.com/news/ct-chicago-state-university-financial-crisis-20160204-story.html>.

Comaroff, J. and Comaroff, J. L. (2000) Millennial capitalism: First thoughts on a second coming. *Public Culture* 12(2): 291–343.

Comaroff, J. and Comaroff, J. L. (2012) *Theory from the South: How Euro-America is Evolving toward Africa*. Boulder, CO: Paradigm.

Connell, R. (2007) *Southern Theory: The Global Dynamics of Knowledge in Social Science*. Cambridge: Polity.

Connors, W. (2014) Google, Microsoft expose Brazil's favelas. *The Wall Street Journal*, 29 September. Available at: <http://www.wsj.com/articles/google-microsoft-expose-brazils-favelas-1411659687>.

Cooke, P. and Morgan, P. (1999) *The Associational Economy: Firms, Regions, and Innovation*. Oxford: Oxford University Press.

Coppola, A. and Vanolo, A. (2015) Normalizing autonomous spaces: Ongoing transformations in Christiania, Copenaghen. *Urban Studies* 52(6): 1152–68.

Crary, J. (2013) *24/7: Late Capitalism and the Ends of Sleep*. London: Verso.

Croce, B. (1921) *Theory and History of Historiography*. London: Harrap & Co. (1st edn 1915).

Croll, E. (2006) *China's New Consumers: Social Development and Domestic Demand*. London: Routledge.

Davies, W. (2015) *The Happiness Industry: How the Government and Big Business Sold us Well-Being*. London: Verso.

Davis, D. S. (2000) Introduction: A revolution in consumption. In Davis, D. S. (ed.) *The Consumer Revolution in Urban China*. Berkeley, CA: University of California Press, pp. 1–24.

Day, E. (2015) #BlackLivesMatter: The birth of a new civil rights movement. *The Guardian*, 19 July. Available at: <https://www.theguardian.com/world/2015/jul/19/blacklivesmatter-birth-civil-rights-movement>.

De Brunhoff, S. (1976) *Marx on Money*. New York: Urizen Books.

Dean, J. (2009) *Democracy and Other Neoliberal Fantasies: Communicative Capitalism and Left Politics*. Durham, NJ: Duke University Press.

Dean, M. (2010) *Governmentality: Power and Rule in Modern Society*. London: Sage.

Dear, M. and Flusty, S. (1998) Postmodern urbanism. *Annals of the Association of American Geographers* 88(1): 50–72.

Debord, G. (1990) *Comments on the Society of the Spectacle*. London: Verso (1st edn 1988).

Deleuze, G. (1992) Postscript on the society of control. *October* 59: 3–7 (1st edn 1990).

Deleuze, G. (1994) *Difference and Repetition*. New York: Columbia University Press (1st edn 1968).

Deleuze, G. and Guattari, F. (1987) *A Thousand Plateaus: Capitalism and Schizophrenia*. Minneapolis, MN: Minnesota University Press (1st edn 1980).

Desmond, D. (2012) Eviction and the reproduction of urban poverty. *American Journal of Sociology* 118(1): 88–133.

Dicken, P. (1986) *The Global Shift: Industrial Change in a Turbulent World*. London: Harper & Row.

Dicken, P. (2011) *The Global Shift: Mapping the Changing Contours of the World Economy*. London: Sage.

Dougherty, C. (2016) In cramped and costly Bay Area, cries to build, baby, build. *The New York Times*, 16 April. Available at: <http://www.nytimes.com/2016/04/17/business/economy/san-francisco-housing-tech-boom-sf-barf.html>.

Douthat, R. (2015) Is Donald Trump a fascist?. *The New York Times*, 3 December. Available at: <http://www.nytimes.com/2015/12/03/opinion/campaign-stops/is-donald-trump-a-fascist.html>.

Drucker, P. (1993) *Postcapitalist Society*. New York: Harper Business.

Dunlap, D. D. (1987) Scrutinizing the legacy of Robert Moses. *The New York Times*, 11 May. Available at: <http://www.nytimes.com/1987/05/11/nyregion/scrutinizing-the-legacy-of-robert-moses.html>.

Economist, The (2009) Turning their backs on the world. 19 February. Available at: <http://www.economist.com/node/13145370>.

Economist, The (2011) Taming Leviathan: Special report on the future of the state. 19 March. Available at: <http://www.economist.com/node/18359896>.

Economist, The (2014) A Cambrian moment: Special report on tech startups. 18 January. Available at: <http://www.economist.com/news/special-report/21593580-cheap-and-ubiquitous-building-blocks-digital-products-and-services-have-caused>.

Economist Intelligence Unit (2012) *Super-sized Cities: China's 13 Megalopolises*. London: The Economist.

Eisenhauer, E. (2001) In poor health: Supermarket redlining and urban nutrition. *GeoJournal* 53(2): 125–33.

Eisinger, P. K. (1988) *The Rise of the Entrepreneurial State: State and Local Economic Development Policy in the United States*. Madison, WI: The University of Wisconsin Press.

Elias, N. (2000) *The Civilizing Process: Sociogenetic and Psycogenetic Investigations*. Oxford: Blackwell (1st edn 1939).

Enright, T. and Rossi , U. (Forthcoming) Ambivalence of the commons. In Miller, B., Jonas, A., Ward, K. and Wilson, D. (eds), *Handbook on Spaces of Urban Politics*. Abingdon: Routledge.

Erikson, E. H. (1994) *Identity: Youth and Crisis*. New York: Norton (1st edn 1968).

Esposito, R. (2012) *Living Thought. The Origins and Actuality of Italian Philosophy*. Stanford, CA: Stanford University Press (1st edn 2010).

Esposito, R. (2016) *Da fuori. Una filosofia per l'Europa*. Turin: Einaudi.

Farinelli, F. (2003) *Geografia: Un'introduzione ai modelli del mondo*. Turin: Einaudi.

Featherstone, M. (1991) *Consumer Culture and Postmodernism*. Thousand Oaks, CA: Sage.

Feng, E. (2016) Skyscrapers' rise in China marks the fall of immigrant enclaves. *The New York Times*, 19 July. Available at: <http://www.nytimes.com/2016/07/20/world/asia/skyscrapers-rise-in-china-mark-the-fall-of-immigrant-enclaves.html?_r=0>.

Ferguson, J. and Gupta, A. (2002) Spatializing states: Toward an ethnography of neoliberal governmentality. *American Ethnologist* 29(4): 981–1002.

Finamore, C. (2016) Black homes matter: San Francisco's vanishing black population. *San Francisco Bay View. National Black Newspaper*, 11 January. Avail-

able at: <http://sfbayview.com/2016/01/black-homes-matter-san-franciscos
-vanishing-black-population/>.

Florida, R. (2002) *The Rise of the Creative Class: And How it's Transforming Work, Leisure, Community, and Everyday Life*. New York: Basic Books.

Florida, R. (2012) *The Rise of the Creative Class – Revised and Expanded*. New York: Basic Books.

Florida, R., Mellander, C. and Rentfrow, P. J. (2013) The happiness of cities. *Regional Studies* 47(4): 613–27.

Florida, R. (2014) *Startup City: The Urban Shift in Venture Capital and High Technology*. Toronto: Martin Prosperity Institute.

Florida, R., Matheson, Z., Adler, P. and Brydges, T. (2014) *The Divided City: And the Shape of the New Metropolis*. Toronto: Martin Prosperity Institute.

Foglesong, R. E. (2001) *Married to the Mouse: Walt Disney World and Orlando*. New Haven, CT: Yale University Press.

Foroohar, R. (2016) American capitalism's great crisis. *Time*, 12 May. Available at: <http://time.com/4327419/american-capitalisms-great-crisis/>.

Foucault, M. (1982) The subject and power. *Critical Inquiry* 8(4): 777–95.

Foucault, M. (1990) *The History of Sexuality. Volume 1: An Introduction*. New York: Vintage (1st edn 1976).

Foucault, M. (1995) *Discipline and Punish: The Birth of the Prison*. New York: Vintage (1st edn 1975).

Foucault, M. (2008), *The Birth of Biopolitics: Lectures at the College de France, 1978–79*. Basingstoke: Palgrave Macmillan (1st edn 2004).

Fourastié, J. (1979) *Les trente glorieuses, ou la révolution invisible de 1946 à 1975*. Paris: Fayard.

French, D. E. (2010) *Walk Away: The Rise and Fall of the Home-ownership Myth*. Auburn, AL: Ludwig von Mises Institute.

Friedmann, J. (1966) *Regional Development Policy: A Case Study of Venezuela*. Cambridge, MA: MIT Press.

Friedmann, J. (1986) The world city hypothesis. *Development and Change* 17(1): 69–83.

Friedmann, J. and Wolff, G. (1982) World city formation: An agenda for research and action. *International Journal of Urban and Regional Research* 6(3): 309–44.

Fujita, K. (2003) Neo-industrial Tokyo: Urban development and globalisation in Japan's state-centred developmental capitalism. *Urban Studies* 40(2): 249–81.

Fukuyama, F. (1997) *Trust: The Social Virtues and the Creation of Prosperity*. New York: Free Press.

Garreau, J. (1991) *Edge City: Life on the New Frontier*. New York: Doubleday.

Giddens, A. (1991) *Modernity and Self-identity: Self and Society in the Late Modern Age*. Cambridge: Polity.

Giddens, A. (1998) *The Third Way: The Renewal of Social Democracy*. Cambridge: Polity.

Glaeser, E. L. (2011) *Triumph of the City: How Our Greatest Invention Makes Us Richer, Smarter, Greener, Healthier and Happier*. New York: Penguin.

Glassman, J. (2006) Primitive accumulation, accumulation by dispossession, accumulation by 'extra-economic means'. *Progress in Human Geography* 30(5): 608–25.

Gómez, M. V. and González, S. (2001) A reply to Beatriz Plaza's 'The Guggenheim-Bilbao museum effect'. *International Journal of Urban and Regional Research* 25(4): 898–900.

González, S. (2006) Scalar narratives in Bilbao: A cultural politics of scale approach to the study of urban policy. *International Journal of Urban and Regional Research* 30(4): 836–57.

González, S. (2011) Bilbao and Barcelona 'in motion': How urban regeneration 'models' travel and mutate in the global flows of policy tourism. *Urban Studies* 48(7): 1397–1418.

Gordon, C. (1991) Governmental rationality: An introduction. In Burchell, G., Gordon, C. and Miller, P. (eds) *Studies in Governmentality*. Chicago, IL: University of Chicago Press, pp. 1–52.

Gordon, D. M., Edwards, R. and Reich, M. (1994) Long swings and stages of capitalism. In Kotz, D. M., McDonough, T. and Reich, M. (eds), *Social Structures of Accumulation: The Political Economy of Growth and Crisis*. Cambridge: Cambridge University Press, pp. 11–28.

Gotham, K. F. (2009) Creating liquidity out of spatial fixity: The secondary circuit of capital and the subprime mortgage crisis. *International Journal of Urban and Regional Research* 33(2): 355–71.

Gottmann, J. (1962) *Megalopolis: The Urbanized Northeastern Seaboard of the United States*. Cambridge, MA: MIT Press.

Greenberg, M. (2008) *Branding New York: How a City in Crisis was Sold to the World*. London: Routledge.

Gross, D. (2009) Globalization slows down. *Newsweek*, 11 December. Available at: <http://europe.newsweek.com/globalization-slows-down-75735?rm=eu>.

Hägerstrand, T. (1967) *Innovation Diffusion as a Spatial Process*. Chicago, IL: University of Chicago Press.

Hall, P. (1998) *Cities in Civilization. Culture, Innovation, and Urban Order*. London: Weidenfield & Nicolson.

Hall, P. and Pain, K. (2006) (eds) *The Polycentric Metropolis: Learning from Mega-city Regions in Europe*. London: Earthscan.

Hall, P. A. and Soskice, D. (2001) (eds) *Varieties of Capitalism: The Institutional Foundations of Comparative Advantage*. Oxford: Oxford University Press.

Hall, T. and Hubbard, P. (1998) (eds) *The Entrepreneurial City: Geographies of Politics, Regime and Representation*. Chichester: Wiley.

Hannerz, U. (1996) *Transnational Connections: Culture, People, Places*. London: Routledge.

Hardt, M. and Negri, A. (1994) *Labor of Dionysus: A Critique of the State-form*. Minneapolis, MN: Minnesota University Press.

Hardt, M. and Negri, A. (2000) *Empire*. Cambridge, MA: Harvard University Press.

Hardt, M. and Negri, A. (2009) *Commonwealth*. Cambridge, MA: Belknap Press of Harvard University Press.

Harvey, D. (1978) The urban process under capitalism. *International Journal of Urban and Regional Research* 2(1–4): 101–31.

Harvey, D. (1982) *The Limits to Capital*. Oxford: Blackwell.

Harvey, D. (1989a) *The Urban Experience*. Baltimore, MA: The Johns Hopkins University Press.

Harvey, D. (1989b) From managerialism to entrepreneurialism: The transformation in urban governance in late capitalism. *Geografiska Annaler B: Human Geography* 71(1): 3–17.

Harvey, D. (1989c) *The Condition of Postmodernity: An Enquiry into the Origins of Cultural Change*. Oxford: Blackwell.

Harvey, D. (2003) *The New Imperialism*. Oxford: Oxford University Press.

Harvey, D. (2010) *A Companion to Marx's Capital*. London: Verso.

Harvey, D. (2012) *Rebel Cities: From the Right to the City to the Urban Revolution*. London: Verso.

Hernandez, J. (2009) Redlining revisited: Mortgage lending patterns in Sacramento 1930–2004. *International Journal of Urban and Regional Research* 33(2): 291–313.

Hodgson, G. M. (2015) *Conceptualizing Capitalism: Institutions, Evolution, Future*. Chicago, IL: University of Chicago Press.

Holgersen, S. (2015) Economic crisis, (creative) destruction, and the current urban condition. *Antipode* 47(3): 689–707.

Huang, Y. (2008) *Capitalism with Chinese Characteristics: Entrepreneurship and the State*. Cambridge: Cambridge University Press.

Huron, A. (2015) Working with strangers in saturated space: Reclaiming and maintaining the urban commons. *Antipode* 47(4): 963–79.

Ingham, G. (2008) *Capitalism*. Cambridge: Polity.

Irwin, N. (2016) Can U.S. remain an island of stability in the global economy? *The New York Times*, 7 January. Available at: <http://www.nytimes.com/

2016/01/08/upshot/can-us-remain-an-island-of-stability-in-the-global
-economy.html>.

Isin, E. F. (2008) Theorizing acts of citizenship. In Isin, E. F. and Nielsen, G. M. (eds), *Acts of Citizenship*. London: Zed Books, pp. 15–43.

Ivory, D., Protess, B. and Bennett, K. (2016) When you dial 911 and Wall Street answers. *The New York Times*, 25 June. Available at: <http://www.nytimes .com/2016/06/26/business/dealbook/when-you-dial-911-and-wall-street -answers.html?_r=0>.

Jacobs, J. (1961) *The Death and Life of Great American Cities*. New York: Random House.

Jacobs, J. (1969) *The Economy of Cities*. New York: Random House.

Jameson, F. (1979) Reification and utopia in mass culture. *Social Text* 1: 130–48.

Jameson, F. (1991) *Postmodernism, or the Cultural Logic of Late Capitalism*. Durham, NC: Duke University Press.

Jameson, F. (2010) *Valences of the Dialectic*. London: Verso.

Jessop, B. (1990) *State Theory: Putting the Capitalist State in its Place*. Cambridge: Polity.

Jessop B. (1994) Post-Fordism and the state. In A. Amin (ed.), *Post-Fordism. A Reader*. Oxford: Blackwell, pp. 251–79.

Jessop, B. (1997) A neo-Gramscian approach to the regulation of urban regimes: Accumulation strategies, hegemonic projects and governance. In Lauria, M. (ed.), *Reconstructing Urban Regime Theory: Regulating Urban Politics in a Global Economy*. Thousand Oaks, CA: Sage, pp. 51–73.

Jessop, B. (2002a) Liberalism, neo-liberalism and urban governance: A state-theoretical perspective. *Antipode* 34(3): 452–72.

Jessop, B. (2002b) *The Future of the Capitalist State*. Cambridge: Polity.

Jessop, B. (2004) Critical semiotic analysis and cultural political economy. *Critical Discourse Studies* 1(2): 159–74.

Jessop, B. (2011) Rethinking the diversity and variability of capitalism. In Lane, C. and Wood, G. (eds), *Capitalist Diversity and Diversity within Capitalism*. London: Routledge, pp. 209–37.

Jessop, B. (2016) Territory, politics, governance and multispatial metagovernance. *Territory, Politics, Governance* 4(1): 8–32.

Jessop, B. and Sum, N.-L. (2000) An entrepreneurial city in action: Hong Kong's emerging strategies in and for (inter)urban competition. *Urban Studies* 37(12): 2287–2313.

Jessop, B., Brenner, N. and Jones, M. (2008) Theorizing socio-spatial relations. *Environment and Planning D: Society and Space* 26(3): 389–401.

Johnson, I. (2013) China's great uprooting: Moving 250 million into cities. *The New York Times*, 15 June. Available at: <http://www.nytimes.com/2013/

06/16/world/asia/chinas-great-uprooting-moving-250-million-into-cities .html?pagewanted=all>.

Jones, C. and Murie, A. (2006) *The Right to Buy: Analysis and Evaluation of a Housing Policy*. Oxford: Blackwell.

Joseph, B. W. (2005) An interview with Paolo Virno. *Grey Room*, 21: 26–37.

Joseph, M. (2002) *Against the Romance of Community*. Minneapolis, MN: University of Minnesota Press.

Joseph, M. (2014) *Debt to Society: Accounting for Life under Capitalism*. Minneapolis, MN: University of Minnesota Press.

Judd, D. R. and Swanstrom, T. (2014) *City Politics: The Political Economy of Urban America*. Boston, MA: Pearson.

Jurgenson, N. (2010) The de-Mcdonaldization of the Internet. In Ritzer, G. (ed.), *The McDonaldization Reader*. Thousand Oaks, CA: Pine Forge Press, pp. 159–70.

Kagan, P. (2016) This is how fascism comes to America. *The Washington Post*, 18 May. Available at: <https://www.washingtonpost.com/opinions/this-is-how -fascism-comes-to-america/2016/05/17/c4e32c58-1c47-11e6-8c7b-6931 e66333e7_story.html>.

Kasperkevic, J. (2016) Co-living – the companies reinventing the idea of room-mates. *Guardian*, 20 March. Available at: <https://www.theguardian.com/ business/2016/mar/20/co-living-companies-reinventing-roommates-open -door-common->.

Katz, B. And Bradley, J. (2013) *The Metropolitan Revolution: How Cities and Metros are Fixing Our Broken Politics and Fragile Economy*. Washington, DC: Brookings Institution Press.

Kaysen, R. (2015) The millennial commune. *The New York Times*, 31 July. Available at: <http://www.nytimes.com/2015/08/02/realestate/the-millen-nial-commune.html>.

Kellner, D. (2005) Frankfurt School. In Kitzer, G. (ed.), *Encyclopedia of Social Theory*. Thousand Oaks, CA: Sage, vol. 2, pp. 290–3.

Khomami, N. and Halliday, J. (2015) Shoreditch cereal killer cafe targeted in anti-gentrification protests. *Guardian*, 27 September. Available at: <https:// www.theguardian.com/uk-news/2015/sep/27/shoreditch-cereal-cafe -targeted-by-anti-gentrification-protesters>.

Kiviat, B. (2010) Rethinking homeownership. Why owning a home may no longer make economic sense. *Time*, 6 September. Available at: <http:// content.time.com/time/covers/0,16641,20100906,00.html>.

Kling, R., Olin, S. and Poster, M. (1991) The emergence of postsuburbia: An introduction. In Kling, R., Olin, S. and Poster, M. (eds), *Postsuburban California: The Transformation of Orange County since World War II*. Berkeley, CA: University of California Press, pp. 1–30.

Krätke, S. (2014) Cities in contemporary capitalism. *International Journal of Urban and Regional Research* 38(5): 1660–70.

Krippner, G. R. (2005) The financialization of the American economy. *Socio-Economic Review* 3(2): 173–208.

Krugman, P. (2015) Voodoo never dies. *The New York Times*, 2 October. Available at: <http://www.nytimes.com/2015/10/02/opinion/voodoo-never-dies.html>.

Landry, C. and Bianchini, F. (1995) *The Creative City*. London: Demos.

Larner, W. (2000) Neo-liberalism: Policy, ideology, governmentality. *Studies in Political Economy* 63: 5–26.

Lazzarato, M. (1994) Berlusconi: l'entrepreneur politique. *Futur Antérieur* 3–4: 23–4.

Lazzarato, M. (2009) Neoliberalism in action: Inequality, insecurity and the reconstitution of the social. *Theory, Culture & Society* 26(6): 109–33.

Lazzarato, M. (2012) *The Making of the Indebted Man: An Essay on the Neoliberal Condition*. Los Angeles, CA: Semiotext(e).

Lazzarato, M. (2014) *Signs and Machines: Capitalism and the Production of Subjectivities*. Los Angeles, CA: Semiotext(e).

Lears, T. J. J. (1985) The concept of cultural hegemony: Problems and possibilities. *American Historical Review* 90(3): 567–93.

Lefebvre, H. (2003) *The Urban Revolution*. Minneapolis, MN: University of Minnesota Press (1st edn 1970).

Lemke, T. (2001) The birth of bio-politics: Michel Foucault's lecture at the Collège de France on neo-liberal governmentality. *Economy and Society* 30(2): 190–207.

Lenin, V. I. (2004) *The Development of Capitalism in Russia*. Honolulu, HI: University Press of the Pacific (1st edn 1899).

Levinson, M. (2006) *The Box: How the Shipping Container Made the World Small and the World Economy Bigger*. Princeton, NJ: Princeton University Press.

Logan, J. R. and Molotch, H. L. (1987) *Urban Fortunes: The Political Economy of Place*. Berkeley, CA: University of California Press.

Longman, P. (2015) Why the economic fates of America's cities diverged. *The Atlantic*, 28 November. Available at: <http://www.theatlantic.com/business/archive/2015/11/cities-economic-fates-diverge/417372/>.

López-Morales, E. J. (2010) Real estate market, state-entrepreneurialism and urban policy in the 'gentrification by ground rent dispossession' of Santiago de Chile. *Journal of Latin American Geography* 9(1): 145–73.

Lordon, F. (2014) *Willing Slaves of Capital: Spinoza and Marx on Desire*. London: Verso (1st edn 2010).

Lukács, G. (1999) *History and Class Consciousness.* Cambridge, MA: MIT Press (1st edn 1923).

Luogo Comune (1993) *Tesi sul nuovo fascismo europeo* 3(4): 6–8.

Luxembourg, R. (2003) *The Accumulation of Capital.* London: Routledge (1st edn 1913).

McCann, E. (2011) Urban policy mobility and global circuits of knowledge. *Annals of the Association of American Geographers* 101(1): 107–30.

McCann, E. and Ward, K. (2010) Relationality/territoriality: Toward a conceptualization of cities in the world. *Geoforum* 41(2): 175–84.

McFarlane, C. (2012) The entrepreneurial slum: Civil society, mobility and the co-production of urban development. *Urban Studies* 49(13): 2795–2816.

Machimura, T. (1992) The urban restructuring process in Tokyo in the 1980s: Transforming Tokyo into a world city. *International Journal of Urban and Regional Research* 16(1): 114–28.

Marazzi, C. (2010) *The Violence of Financial Capitalism.* Los Angeles, CA: Semiotext(e).

Marazzi, C. (2011) *Capital and Affects: The Politics of the Language Economy.* Los Angeles, CA: Semiotext(e).

Marazzi, C. (2012) *Capital and Language: From the New Economy to the War Economy.* Los Angeles, CA: Semiotext(e).

Marcuse, H. (1991) *One-Dimensional Man: Studies in the Ideology of Advanced Industrial Society.* London and New York: Penguin (1st edn 1964).

Marinetto, M. (2003) Who wants to be an active citizen? The politics and practice of community investment. *Sociology* 37(1): 103–20.

Martin, R. (2002) *The Financialization of Daily Life.* Philadelphia, PA: Temple University Press.

Marx, K. (1973) *Grundrisse: Introduction to the Critique of Political Economy.* New York: Random House (1st edn 1857–58).

Mason, P. (2015) *Postcapitalism: A Guide to Our Future.* London: Allen Lane.

Massad, J. A. (2015) *Islam in Liberalism.* Chicago, IL: University of Chicago Press.

Mitchell, T. (2011) *Carbon Democracy: Political Power in the Age of Oil.* London: Verso.

Moretti, E. (2012) *The New Geography of Jobs.* Boston, MA: Mariner Books.

Mukhija, V. (2003) *Squatters as Developers? Slum Demolition and Redevelopment in Mumbai.* Aldershot: Ashgate.

Nathan, M. and Vandore, E. (2014) Here be start-ups: Exploring London's 'Tech City' digital cluster. *Environment and Planning A* 46(10): 2283–99.

National Commission (2011) *The Financial Crisis Inquiry Report.* Washington, DC: Official Government Edition.

Negri, A. (1989) *Marx beyond Marx: Lessons on the Grundrisse.* New York: Autonomedia (1st edn 1979).

Negri, A. (1991) *The Savage Anomaly: The Power of Spinoza's Metaphysics and Politics.* Minneapolis, MN: University of Minnesota Press (1st edn 1981).

O'Connor, J. (1973) *The Fiscal Crisis of the State.* New York: St Martin's Press.

Ohmae, K. (1990) *The Borderless World: Power and Strategy in the Interlinked Economy.* London: Collins.

Ong, A. (2006) *Neoliberalism as Exception: Mutations in Citizenship and Sovereignty.* Durham, NC: Duke University Press.

Ong, A. (2007) Neoliberalism as a mobile technology. *Transactions of the Institute of British Geographers* 32(1): 3–8.

Patel, R. (2007) *Stuffed and Starved: Markets, Power and the Hidden Battle for the World Food System.* London: Portobello Books.

Patel, R. (2010) *The Value of Nothing: How to Reshape Market Society and Redefine Democracy.* New York: Picador.

Peck, J. (2001) Neoliberalizing states: Thin policies/hard outcomes. *Progress in Human Geography* 25(3): 445–55.

Peck, J. (2010) *Constructions of Neoliberal Reason.* New York: Oxford University Press.

Peck, J. (2012) Austerity urbanism. *City* 16(6): 626–55.

Peck, J. (2015) Cities beyond compare? *Regional Studies* 49(1): 160–82.

Peck, J. and Theodore, N. (2007) Variegated capitalism. *Progress in Human Geography* 31(6): 731–72.

Peck, J. and Theodore, N. (2015) *Fast Policy: Experimental Statecraft at the Threshold of Neoliberalism.* Minneapolis, MN: University of Minnesota Press.

Peck, J. and Zhang, J. (2013) A variety of capitalism … with Chinese characteristics? *Journal of Economic Geography* 13(3): 357–96.

Pelkonen, A. (2005) State restructuring, urban competitiveness policies and technopole building in Finland: A critical view on the glocal state thesis. *European Planning Studies* 13(5): 685–705.

Perelman, M. (2000) *The Invention of Capitalism: Classical Political Economy and the Secret History of Primitive Accumulation.* Durham, NC: Duke University Press.

Peterson, P. (1981) *City Limits.* Chicago, IL: University of Chicago Press.

Philippe, D. (2006) Nicolas Sarkozy veut faire de la France 'un pays de propriétaires'. *Le Moniteur.fr*, 12 December. Available at: <http://www.lemoniteur.fr/article/nicolas-sarkozy-veut-faire-de-la-france-un-pays-de-proprietaires-75473>.

Piketty, T. (2014) *Capital in the Twenty-First Century*. Cambridge, MA: Belknap Press.

Piore, M. and Sabel, C. (1984) *The Second Industrial Divide: Possibilities for Prosperity*. New York: Basic Books.

Pirenne, H. (1956) *Medieval Cities: Their Origins and the Revival of Trade*. Princeton, NJ: Princeton University Press (1st edn 1925).

Polanyi, K. (2001) *The Great Transformation: The Political and Economic Origins of Our Time*. Boston, MA: Beacon Press (1st edn 1944).

Ponzini, D. (2011) Large-scale development projects and star architecture in the absence of democratic politics: The case of Abu Dhabi, UAE. *Cities* 28(3): 251–9.

Ponzini, D. and Rossi, U. (2010) Becoming a creative city: The entrepreneurial mayor, network politics and the promise of an urban renaissance. *Urban Studies* 47(5): 1037–57.

Porter, M. (1985) *Competitive Advantage: Creating and Sustaining Superior Performance*. New York: Simon and Schuster.

Povinelli, E. (2011) *Economies of Abandonment: Social Belonging and Endurance in Late Liberalism*. Durham, NC: Duke University Press.

Purcell, M. (2013) *The Down-deep Delight of Democracy*. Malden, MA: Wiley-Blackwell.

Putnam, R. (1993) *Making Democracy Work: Civic Traditions in Modern Italy*. Princeton, NJ: Princeton University Press.

Putnam, R. (2000) *Bowling Alone: The Collapse and Revival of American Community*. New York: Simon & Schuster.

Reba, M., Reitsma, F. and K. C. Seto (2016) Spatializing 6,000 years of global urbanization from 3700 BC to AD 2000. *Scientific Data* 3, doi: 10.1038/sdata.2016.34.

Reinhart, C. M. and Rogoff, K. S. (2009) *This Time is Different: Eight Centuries of Financial Folly*. Princeton, NJ: Princeton University Press.

Richburg, K. B. (2010) Disneyland project in Shanghai spotlights forced evictions in China. *The Washington Post*, 19 June. Available at: <http://www.washingtonpost.com/wp-dyn/content/article/2010/06/18/AR2010061805277.html>.

Rickards, L., Gleeson, B., Boyle, M. and O'Callaghan, C. (2016) Urban studies after the age of the city. *Urban Studies* 53(8): 1523–41.

Rifkin, J. (2004) *The European Dream: How Europe's Vision of the Future is Quietly Eclipsing the American Dream*. Cambridge: Polity.

Rifkin, J. (2014) *The Zero Marginal Cost Society*. New York: Palgrave Macmillan.

Ritzer, G. (1983) The 'McDonaldization' of society. *Journal of American Culture* 6(1): 100–7.

Ritzer, G. and Jurgenson, N. (2010) Production, consumption, prosumption: The nature of capitalism in the age of the 'digital prosumer'. *Journal of Consumer Culture* 10(1): 10–36.

Robinson, J. (2006) *Ordinary Cities: Between Modernity and Development*. London: Routledge.

Robinson, J. (2011) Cities in a world of cities: The comparative gesture. *International Journal of Urban and Regional Research* 35(1): 1–23.

Robinson, J. (2016) Thinking cities through elsewhere: Comparative tactics for a more global urban studies. *Progress in Human Geography* 40(1): 3–29.

Rodríguez-Pose, A. (2008) The rise of the 'city-region' concept and its development policy implications. *European Planning Studies* 16(8): 1025–46.

Ronald, R. (2008) *Homeownership: Homeowner Societies and the Role of Housing*. Basingstoke: Palgrave Macmillan.

Rossi, U. (2010a) The capitalist city. In Hutchison, R. (ed.), *Encyclopedia of Urban Studies*. Los Angeles, CA: Sage, vol. 1, pp. 109–12.

Rossi, U. (2010b) Manuel Castells. In Hutchison, R. (ed.), *Encyclopedia of Urban Studies*. Los Angeles, CA: Sage, vol. 1, pp. 114–99.

Rossi, U. (2013a) On the varying ontologies of capitalism: Embeddedness, dispossession, subsumption. *Progress in Human Geography*, 37(3): 348–65.

Rossi U. (2013b) On life as a fictitious commodity: Cities and the biopolitcs of late neoliberalism. *International Journal of Urban and Regional Research* 37(3): 1067–74.

Rossi, U. (2016) The variegated economics and the potential politics of the smart city. *Territory, Politics, Governance* 4(3): 337–53.

Rossi, U. (Forthcoming) Neoliberalism. In Jayne, M. and Ward, K. (eds), *Urban Theory: New Critical Perspectives*. Abingdon: Routledge.

Rossi, U. and Vanolo, A. (2012) *Urban Political Geographies: A Global Perspective*. London: Sage.

Roy, A. (2009) The 21st-century metropolis: New geographies of theory. *Regional Studies* 43(6): 819–30.

Roy, A. (2011) Slumdog cities: Rethinking subaltern urbanism. *International Journal of Urban and Regional Research* 35(2): 223–38.

Sassen, S. (1991) *The Global City: New York, London, Tokyo*. Princeton, NJ: Princeton University Press.

Sassen, S. (1994) *Cities in a World Economy*. Thousand Oaks, CA: Pine Forge Press.

Sassen, S. (2014) *Expulsions. Brutality and Complexity in the Global Economy*. Cambridge, MA: Harvard University Press.

Sassen-Koob, S. (1986) New York City: Economic restructuring and immigration. *Development and Change* 17(1): 85–119.

Saunders, P. (1990) *A Nation of Homeowners*. London: Unwin Hyman.

Scholz, T. (2016) *Platform Cooperativism: Challenging the Corporate Sharing Economy*. New York: Rosa Luxembourg Stiftung.

Schulman, B. J. (1991) *From Cotton Belt to Sunbelt: Federal Policy, Economic Development, and the Transformation of the South, 1938–1980*. New York: Oxford University Press.

Schumpeter, J. A. (1939) *Business Cycles: A Theoretical, Historical, and Statistical Analysis of the Capitalist Process*. Chevy Chase, MD: Bartelby Books.

Scott, A. J. (1988) High technology industry and territorial development: The rise of the Orange County complex, 1955–1988. *Urban Geography* 7(1): 3–45.

Scott, A. J. (2001) Globalization and the rise of city-regions. *European Planning Studies* 9(7): 813–26.

Scott A. J. (2006) Creative cities: Conceptual issues and policy questions. *Journal of Urban Affairs* 28(1): 1–7.

Scott, A. J. (2008) *Social Economy of the Metropolis: Cognitive-cultural Capitalism and the Global Resurgence of Cities*. Oxford: Oxford University Press.

Scott, A. J. (2014) Beyond the creative city: Cognitive-cultural capitalism and the new urbanism, *Regional Studies* 48(4): 565–78.

Scott, A. J. and Storper, M. (2015) The nature of cities: The scope and limits of urban theory. *International Journal of Urban and Regional Research* 39(1): 1–15.

Sennett, R. (1976) *The Fall of Public Man*. Cambridge: Cambridge University Press.

Sennett, R. (1998) *The Corrosion of Character: The Personal Consequences of Work in the New Capitalism*. New York: Norton.

Sheppard, E. J., Leitner, H. and Maringanti, A. (2013) Provincializing global urbanism: A manifesto. *Urban Geography* 34(7): 893–900.

Shirk, S. L. (1993) *The Political Logic of Economic Reform in China*. Berkeley, CA: University of California Press.

Short, R., Breitbach, C., Buckman, S. and Essex, J. (2000) From world cities to gateway cities: Extending the boundaries of globalization theory. *City* 4(3): 317–40.

Sites, W. (2010) Progressive city. In Hutchison, R. (ed.), *Encyclopedia of Urban Studies*. Los Angeles, CA: Sage, vol. 2, pp. 610–13.

Sklair, L. (1991) *Sociology of the Global System*. New York: Harvester Wheatsheaf.

Smet, K. (2016) Housing prices in urban areas. *Progress in Human Geography* 40(4): 495–510.

Smith, M. P. (2001) *Transnational Urbanism: Locating Globalization*. Malden, MA: Blackwell.

Smith, M. P. and Feagin, J. R. (1987) (eds) *The Capitalist City: Global Restructuring and Community Politics*. Oxford: Blackwell.

Soja, E. W. (2000) *Postmetropolis: Critical Studies of Cities and Regions*. Oxford: Blackwell.

Solomon Guggenheim Foundation, The (2011) *Concept and Development Study for a Guggenheim Helsinki*. New York: Guggenheim Museum Publications.

Sorkin, M. (1992) See you in Disneyland. *Design Quarterly* 154: 5–13.

Squires, G. (2004) (ed.) *Why the Poor Pay More: How to Stop Predatory Lending*. Westport, CT: Praeger.

Srnicek, N. (2016) *Platform Capitalism*. Cambridge: Polity.

Srnicek, N. and Williams, A. (2015) *Inventing the Future: Postcapitalism and a World without Work*. London: Verso.

Stallwood, O. (2012) How Berlin is fighting back against growing anti-tourist feeling in the city. *Guardian*, 4 December. Available at: <https://www.theguardian.com/travel/2012/dec/04/berlin-fights-anti-hipster-tourism-abuse>.

Stein, J. (2015) Tales from the sharing economy. *Time*, 9 February. Available at: <http://time.com/3687335/in-the-latest-issue-21/>.

Steinmetz, K. (2014) San Francisco's new disruption. *Time*, 31 January. Available at: <http://time.com/2852/disrupted/>.

Steinmetz, K. (2016a) Inside Airbnb's plan to build a grassroots political movement. *Time*, 21 July. Available at: <http://time.com/4416136/airbnb-politics-sharing-economy-regulations-housing/>.

Steinmetz, K. (2016b) See how big the gig economy really is. *Time*, 6 January. Available at: <http://time.com/4169532/sharing-economy-poll/>.

Storper, M. (1993) Regional 'worlds' of production: Learning and innovation in the technology districts of France, Italy and the USA. *Regional Studies* 27(5): 433–55.

Storper, M. (1995) The resurgence of regions ten years later: The region as a nexus of untraded interdependences. *European Urban and Regional Studies* 2(3): 191–221.

Storper, M. (2013) *Keys to the City: How Economics, Social Interaction, and Politics Shape Development*. Princeton, NJ: Princeton University Press.

Storper, M. and Scott, A. J. (2009) Rethinking human capital, creativity and urban growth. *Journal of Economic Geography* 9(2): 147–67.

Strauss, K. (2009) Accumulation and dispossession: Lifting the veil on the sub-prime mortgage crisis. *Antipode* 41(1): 10–14.

Sugrue, T. J. (1996) *The Origins of the Urban Crisis: Race and Inequality in Postwar Detroit*. Princeton, NJ: Princeton University Press.

Summers, L. H. (2014) U.S. economic prospects: Secular stagnation, hysteresis, and the zero lower bound. *Business Economics* 49: 65–73.

Swarns, R. L. (2015) Biased lending evolves, and blacks face trouble getting mortgages. *The New York Times*, 30 October. Available at: <http://www.nytimes.com/2015/10/31/nyregion/hudson-city-bank-settlement.html>.

Swyngedouw, E. (1992) Neither global nor local: 'Glocalization' and the politics of scale. In Cox, K. (ed.), *Spaces of Globalization: Reasserting the Power of the Local*. New York: Guilford Press, pp. 137–66.

Swyngedouw, E. (2005) Governance innovation and the citizen: The Janus face of governance-beyond-the-state. *Urban Studies* 42(11): 1991–2006.

Tandy Shermer, E. (2011) Sunbelt boosterism: Industrial recruitment, economic development, and growth politics in the developing sunbelt. In Nickerson, M. and Dochuck, D. (eds), *Sunbelt Rising: The Politics of Space, Place and Region*. Philadelphia, PA: University of Pennsylvania Press, pp. 31–57.

Taylor, P. J. (1995) World cities and territorial states: The rise and fall of their mutuality. In Knox, P. L. and Taylor, P. J. (eds), *World Cities in a World-System*. Cambridge: Cambridge University Press, pp. 48–62.

Taylor, P. J. (2000) World cities and territorial states under conditions of globalization. *Political Geography* 19(1): 5–32.

Taylor, P. J. (2004) *World City Network: A Global Urban Analysis*. London: Routledge.

Thompson, E. P. (1963) *The Making of the English Working Class*. London: Gollancz.

Thrift N. J. (2005) *Knowing Capitalism*. London: Sage.

Tomba, M. (2009) Historical temporalities of capital: An anti-historicist perspective. *Historical Materialism* 17(4): 44–65.

Törnqvist, G. (2011) *The Geography of Creativity*. Cheltenham: Edward Elgar.

Toscano, A. (2008) The open secret of real abstraction. *Rethinking Marxism* 20(2): 273–87.

Turner, R. S. (1992) Growth politics and downtown development: The economic imperative in sunbelt cities. *Urban Affairs Review* 28(1): 3–21.

Uitermark, J. (2015) Looking for Wikitopia: The study and politics of self-organization. *Urban Studies* 52(13): 2301–12.

US Department of Housing and Urban Development (1995) *The National Homeownership Strategy: Partners in the American Dream*. Washington, DC.

van der Zwan, N. (2014) Making sense of financialization. *Socio-Economic Review* 12(1): 99–129.

Van Maanen, J. (1992) Displacing Disney: Some notes on the flow of culture. *Qualitative Sociology* 15(1): 5–35.

Vanolo, A. (2014) Smartmentality: The smart city as disciplinary strategy. *Urban Studies* 51(5): 883–98.

Vattimo, G. and Zabala, S. (2011) *Hermeneutic Communism: From Heidegger to Marx*. New York: Columbia University Press.

Vercellone, C. (2008) The new articulation of wages, rent and profit in cognitive capitalism. Paper presented at the Queen Mary University School of Management, London. Available at: <https://halshs.archives-ouvertes.fr/halshs-00265584/>.

Viita, K. (2014) Down and out in post-Nokia Finland. *Bloomberg Business*, 7 August. Available at: <http://www.bloomberg.com/news/articles/2014-08-07/nokia-decline-finlands-tech-workers-face-bleak-job-market>.

Virno, P. (1996a) Do you remember counterrevoluton?. In Hardt, M. and Virno, P. (eds), *Radical Thought in Italy: A Potential Politics*. Minneapolis, MN: Minnesota University Press, pp. 241–60.

Virno, P. (1996b) The ambivalence of disenchantement. In Hardt, M. and Virno, P. (eds), *Radical Thought in Italy: A Potential Politics*. Minneapolis, MN: Minnesota University Press, pp. 13–36.

Virno, P. (2007) General intellect. *Historical Materialism* 15(3): 3–8.

Virno, P. (2015) L'usage de la vie. *Multitudes* 58: 143–58.

Volner, I. (2015) Can the Guggenheim charm Finland? *The New Yorker*, 12 May. Available at: <http://www.newyorker.com/culture/culture-desk/can-the-guggenheim-charm-finland>.

Wachsmuth, D. (2014) Post-city politics: US urban governance and competitive multi-city regionalism. Unpublished PhD thesis, New York University.

Wacquant, L. (2012) Three steps to a historical anthropology of actually existing neoliberalism. *Social Anthropology* 20(1): 66–79.

Wallerstein, I. (1979) *The Capitalist World-System*. Cambridge: Cambridge University Press.

Ward, K. (2006) 'Policies in motion', urban management, state restructuring: The trans-local expansion of Business Improvement Districts. *International Journal of Urban and Regional Research* 30(1): 54–75.

Ward, K. (2010) Towards a relational comparative approach to the study of cities. *Progress in Human Geography* 34(4): 471–87.

Wauters, R. (2012) Airbnb: 5 million nights booked, opening 6 new international offices. *TechCrunch*, 26 January. Available at: <https://techcrunch.com/2012/01/26/airbnb-5-million-nights-booked-opening-6-new-international-offices-in-q1-2012/>.

Weber, M. (2001) *The Protestant Ethic and the Spirit of Capitalism*. London: Routledge (1st edn 1904–5).

Wiig, A. (2016) The empty rhetoric of the smart city: From digital inclusion to economic promotion in Philadelphia. *Urban Geography* 37(4): 535–53.

Wu, F. (2003) The (post-) socialist entrepreneurial city as a state project: Shanghai's reglobalisation in question. *Urban Studies* 40(9): 1673–98.

Yan, Y. (2006) McDonald's in Beijing: The localization of Americana. In Watson, J. L. (ed.), *Golden Arches East: McDonald's in East Asia*. Stanford, CA: Stanford University Press, pp. 39–76.

Young, I. M. (1990) *Justice and the Politics of Difference*. Princeton, NJ: Princeton University Press.

Žižek, S. (2008) *The Sublime Object of Ideology*. London: Verso (1st edn 1989).

Zukin, S. (2010) *Naked City: The Death and Life of Authentic Urban Places*. New York: Oxford University Press.

Zukin, S., Lindeman, S. and Hurson, L. (2015) The omnivore's neighbourhood? Online restaurant reviews, race, and gentrification. *Journal of Consumer Culture*, doi:10.1177/1469540515611203.

Index